Best
Dressed

Best Dressed

the **BORN TO SHOP** *lady's*

secrets for building a wardrobe

SUZY GERSHMAN

THREE RIVERS PRESS
NEW YORK

Published by Three Rivers Press, New York, New York. Member of the Crown Publishing Group.

Random House, Inc. New York, Toronto, London, Sydney, Auckland
www.randomhouse.com

THREE RIVERS PRESS is a registered trademark of Random House, Inc.

Originally published in hardcover by Clarkson Potter/Publishers in 1999.

Printed in the United States of America

Design by Maggie Hinders

Library of Congress Cataloging-in-Publication Data
Gershman, Suzy.
    Best dressed: the born to shop lady's secrets to building a wardrobe / by Suzy Gershman. — 1st ed.
    1. Clothing and dress.   2. Fashion.   I. Title.
TT507.G47   1999
646'.34—dc21   98-45726

ISBN 0-609-80581-9

10 9 8 7 6 5 4 3 2 1

First Paperback Edition

Acknowledgments

Hugs and handbags filled with thanks go to my editor, Pamela Krauss, who created this book from thin air—I never would have done it without her help and guidance. Thank-yous also to my agent, Alice Martell, for her patience and sense of humor, and my husband, Michael Gershman, for his unending support. The folks at the FIT Library in New York and all my inside sources helped provide the finishing touches and details. Thanks one and all.

Contents

Best
Dressed

Introduction

I may have been Born to Shop, but I was also born right after World War II. Yep, I am a baby boomer. I came of age in the 1960s, which actually has a lot to do with this book. Everything relevant to today's world of fashion, consumerism, and smart buying is an outgrowth of what happened in the fashion and retail business in the sixties.

And while I personally never felt I was part of the remarkable events of that time, I now realize I have indeed been part of the revolution. For shoppers, it wasn't the hippie revolution or the rock and roll revolution or the free sex revolution that set us free; it was the retail revolution.

The truth is, many of the most important moments in fashion—and in my fashion education—happened when I was in high school, college, and just starting out in fashion in New York.

You see, in high school I was 5'11" tall. This was a terrible burden in both the social and fashion realms. All the "in" girls dressed head to toe in Bobbi Brooks, a popular midpriced designer label of

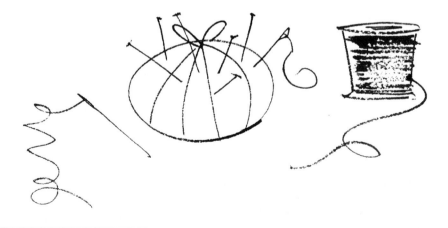

the day that simply did not fit me because of my unconventional proportions.

Of course, even if Bobbi Brooks clothes had fit me, my family rarely shopped at full retail anyway, for both economic and philosophical reasons, so I would have never had the closet full of Bobbi Brooks that I craved. My wardrobe generally consisted of one new dress each season, a few items from bargain bins, and a lot of hand-me-downs.

Since I couldn't simply buy what I wanted, I went to North Star Mall and enrolled in the Singer Sewing class, where I learned to copy Bobbi Brooks looks expertly and to tailor them to fit me.

As I moved past Bobbi Brooks and into my Carnaby Street period, I began to seek out alternative resources and bargains, creating my own take on the important looks of the moment as best I could. My high school yearbook features a photo of me proudly resplendent in my Mary Quant wannabe dress.

While I no longer sew many of my own clothes, the knowledge of garment construction that I acquired from my sewing classes at North Star Mall remains a fundamental in my life today...and the taste of victory I got from off-price shopping in the bins at Solo-Serve when I'd make a real score continues to inspire my quest for bigger and better bargains.

The Bobbi Brooks people did just fine without me. As it happens, Bobbi Brooks was the first garment company to go public, thus signaling a permanent change in the economics of fashion. Throughout my coming-of-age in the fashion world, I watched fashion evolve from a small, boutique industry into big business.

Through the luck of timing, I had the good fortune to know and watch Anne Klein create sportswear that lived and breathed and had a designer touch; I saw Calvin Klein launch his business. Hey, I knew Ralph Lauren when he made ties. I knew Halston well enough to call him Roy—honest. Giorgio di Sant Angelo used to lend me clothes to wear to parties, and I spoke bad French to

Oscar de la Renta's first wife, Françoise. I mention all this because by being born in the right time, as Paul Simon would say, has made me part of the whole picture and fully able to see what's happened to retail and where fashion and consumer trends are going.

Yet there are generations of consumers who have not learned much more than superficial fashion and shopping basics, who aren't aware there was a revolution in their closets.

A lot of today's consumers are shopping in a black hole, forced to rely on the false security of designer labels not only because of the status they imply but because they know nothing about construction and quality and therefore lack confidence in their own buying skills.

Luckily, it's never too late to learn. While you may not be willing to hie yourself down to the local mall to sign up for a Singer sewing class, there's a wealth of knowledge to be shared, and it's on display everywhere from tony boutiques and high-end department stores to the final markdown rack at Filene's Basement. I'm not just Born to Shop, I've made a science *and* an art of it for thirty years. Now I'm here to pass on all the tricks of the trade I have accumulated from traveling (and shopping) around the globe, from working in the fashion industry, from writing the Born to Shop series for more than a dozen years, and from spending hundreds of hours happily pursuing the ultimate bargain.

It's taken me years to get my wardrobe to a place where I can calmly and confidently reach into my closet and pull out an ensemble that not only makes me look good but makes me feel good—no matter what unexpected occasion presents itself. I didn't put a wardrobe like this together overnight, and neither will you, but I believe that information is power. With this book in hand you'll be able to accurately assess your current fashion standing and take control of your shopping habits so that you can:

- stop making costly or embarrassing mistakes.
- define and refine your personal style.
- hone your bargain sense to make your shopping dollars go twice as far.
- gain a new confidence about yourself and your look.

In the chapters that follow I will pull apart the psychology of shopping and image building, then reveal all the layers and levels and little secrets of retail. After that, it's off to the mall, your favorite stores and specialty boutiques, even mail-order catalogs and factory outlets in search of the good sense and true friends that will make you look your best all of the time. We are going to sharpen your already good survival skills and turn you into a smarter shopper, a better consumer, and, most important, a better-dressed woman. After that, you're on your own— a lean, mean shopping machine.

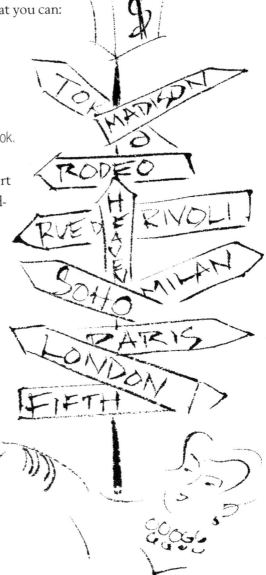

chapter 1

You Are What You Wear

What Your Wardrobe Says About You

No matter how far above the fashion fray you like to imagine yourself—no fashion victims here!—the clothes you don each day make very telling statements about who you are and how you think, the culture you grew up in, and which values you accept and reject. Forget that old hippie saying, you are what you eat. In the modern world, you are what you wear.

At least, you are what you wear while you are wearing it. And that's the secret. We all know that clothing can change how we look and even how we feel, but few of us are willing to take control to make clothing work for us, to tell others how to feel about us.

How you shop, how you perceive your trophy, how you enjoy your purchases are all a part of the big picture. We all understand the relationship between food and figure, yet few people correlate their shopping patterns and what they look like to a food plan. It takes a lot of discipline to keep your figure over a period of years; it takes just as much discipline to keep a wardrobe looking smart over the years. Eat a lot of junk food and you eventually get fat, sure; *buy* a lot of junk and you will surely begin to look bad. It's just that simple. And just as we eat for more than the simple purpose of staving off starvation, we dress for reasons more complicated than just the need to cover our nakedness.

However, clothes and accessories don't come in vending machines and aren't sold at drive-thru eateries; they do not come with a list of ingredients or warnings about what they can do to your image if worn in the wrong manner. So protecting your image is even harder than keeping your figure…and there's a lot less help and support out there.

Yes, we change over the years; our shopping styles also change over the years, reflecting economics, varying environments, gathered wisdom, and what you can borrow from your sister. A healthy lifestyle or way of eating can last a lifetime; to keep a wardrobe healthy, it too must be modified regularly. But the underlying fact remains a staple one: each day when we get up and put on clothes to cover our nakedness, we have the chance to reinvent ourselves.

Napoleon once said that an army marches on its belly and insisted that his men be well fed in order to conquer the world. I feel the same way about my closet and what's inside it. I need good working tools in order to do my best, to look my best. Today's woman marches on her image. However, every day when you face the music—in your closet—you can only come face-to-face with your own shopping habits (good ones and bad ones) and your own triumphs or disasters. The ammunition that you have to work with is all right there before you…and you are the main person who supplied it. Aside from a few hand-me-downs and gifts, you bought all that stuff: the good, the bad, and the ugly.

The manner in which you accumulated this wealth is as important, because you cannot do battle without the right ammunition, and indeed, the fight to look your best only gets easier when you have a system that works for you and keeps you smart, well supplied, and on your toes. We all know that Mother was right when she said money didn't grow on clothes-trees, so the funds we have for the battles must be used to maximum advantage.

Economic Truths

In our crazy economy, many people think that clothing and price are so interwoven that they lose sight of the cost of a real wardrobe. Some even have the misconception that a bargain is solely related to price as if the lowest price paid for an item wins a prize. The real truth: *a bargain is defined by the relationship of quality and value to the time and trouble it took you to acquire the item.*

Call me Madame Einstein.

There are plenty of people who are comfortable walking into a store, shopping carefully, and paying full retail for the items they select. Many of them consider themselves smart shoppers; some will even tell you that they got a bargain by using this method, as they wear their clothes for years.

Others were weaned on the mantra "never pay full price" and hardly ever set foot in department stores. They don't look at clothes that aren't discounted or marked down, they feel cheated if they don't get "a deal," and they can recite a life list of their best finds. They too consider themselves smart shoppers, even though they may dispose of these so-called bargains after only one season, reasoning that the investment was modest, the item has served its purpose.

...ther shopping style can be effective; *the goal is to simply look* ...*best.*

es

...us is born with a credit card in our hands, shopping ...uired skill that evolves gradually over time. There will be aspects of your shopping style that you learned from your mother in your earliest years just as you will probably reject some of her shopping habits simply because you hated that your mother did them. Some of your choices will be influenced by what you pick up from magazines and music videos, from travel (domestic and foreign), and from street fashions. Yet other lessons will be learned from mistakes—sometimes costly ones—and by demands of your peer group.

Never underestimate the power and the pressure exerted by a peer group—at all ages in your life. I'm not just talking to teenagers here: we all have peer groups; they simply change as our stage of life changes.

Work in a big company where you are committing fashion hari-kari if you look different from everyone else? Go with the flow and understand and internalize that dress code, if only for this part of your life.

To thine ownself be true—sure, but more important:

Know the lay of the land. Learn the lingo of the unspoken. Learn the power of a glance. Fall into the knowledge that you can control illusion and use it as information. Wearing the right thing for you *and* for the situation is the only way to achieve personal power in dressing. Don't separate the two parts of the equation.

Fashion should be fun because it is a way to express who you are and who you want the world to think you are. We *do* judge a book by its cover, and that's a fact. What you wear immediately tells the outside world of on-gazers who you are, or *who you want them to think you are*. By making smart wardrobe choices you can fool some of the people some of the time. Being "best dressed" comes from having a strong sense not only of yourself but of what's right in your environment and how you merge those two. Confidence comes from a successful merge. Which brings me to:

You will always feel your best in clothes that you know your peers admire.

The Marie Curie Theorem of Shopping

In the real world of business and commerce, clothes and costume merge just as academic and emotional shopping merge. Clothes therefore should be used to convey far more than the fact that you aren't naked and that you are warm enough. Accordingly, shopping for clothes should be done with a scientific approach.

Yes, clothes should express your personality, but that is actually a secondary point. Honest. *Number Two.*

Here's Number One:

The right clothes are right because they make the people who gaze upon you comfortable with what they see.

Yeah, that's the secret of life. And fashion. And confidence.

You cannot be taller or younger or richer or smarter, but you can make people think you are all these things by the way you dress.

Making Good Choices

From the rational part of my brain, the part that has studied retail for decades, I can tell you—and tell you without hesitation—that there is a simple, happy-go-lucky rule to shopping that will turn you into a winner just about every time you go for a shopping spree: The most efficient way to maximize your fashion dollars is to shop at big department store sales, buying only those items on second markdowns that will work with your existing wardrobe. I call this Retail Rule Number One.

Buying regular retail stock on second markdown is the biggest, and usually best, fashion bargain.

This piece of wisdom is on a par with those handed down by your parents, when your father taught you to hold on 15 in blackjack and your mother said there's no such thing as a little bit pregnant. In fact, so certain am I that this is the basic shopper's gospel that I would even say that if you don't live in a big metropolitan area with lots of department stores and shopping choices, you should save your hard-earned bucks and fly into a city like L.A., San Francisco, Dallas, Chicago, or New York (New York being best of the bunch) once or twice a year and do a fistful of shopping in one big haul. At second markdown, of course.

But, alas, a brain has more than one side, a personality has many facets, a woman has two feet. Nothing is as simple as it appears to be. So the other side of my brain shudders at the thought of such dispassionate disbursements, bemoans a life spent only in department stores…can't hold on 15 all of the time, even if it *is* the sensible thing to do.

Do I shop only at department store sales? Nope! I'm far too emotional.

And shopping can be a very emotional subject.

Rule Number One is for people who want to play it safe.

Those of us who are willing to take risks are just as likely to pop off to the mall, the discount store, the factory outlets, the designer sample sales, and the tag sales, waiting to be confronted with choices…daring the system to bear down just a little bit so we can find more selection, better price, bigger bargains in an offbeat place.

There will always be a disparity between what your brain tells you and what your heart tells you. I find that when I shop safe I may get good buys or make smart choices, but I'm rarely thrilled with the purchases—they don't zing inside my soul. For me, a home run has to hit a number of bases, and being sensibly practical does not give me chills. When I come home with something that gives me an emotional lift *and* makes good wardrobe and financial sense, that I can't wait to haul out of the bag and try on again, that I can't wait to actually wear: that's a good day of shopping.

Which is not to say that every purchase has to be a Find with a capital *F;* you can't build a functional wardrobe by shopping emotionally. But you can't be too rigid about it either. The best shopping decisions marry the emotional and the dispassionate.

Your Personal Shopping Style

We've all looked at a closet filled with clothes and moaned, "I haven't got a thing to wear." Why do we laugh, knowing it's all too possible? Because we don't shop as well as we dress.

Unless you wear a uniform, or have such a highly evolved and

distinctive style that 90 percent of the choices out there in stores and catalogs are automatically eliminated, you shop for your own clothes and you put them together to present yourself to the world. The more you like to shop, the greater the chances that you will be tempted to mix and match, to experiment and to create.

Don't confuse your Personal Style with your Shopping Style. Personal Style is what you look like when you're finished. Shopping Style is how you get there.

The world's most fashion-forward women create their own styles before they become a style, taking a little of this and a little of that and putting it together in a unique manner. Somehow, it works and even evolves into a trend or style that others will imitate. These women are usually in the fashion business or an artistic field that allows, and encourages, these statements. But no one creates a look without the ammunition to do so—and the ammunition is provided by shopping trips, whether to flea markets, designer showrooms, or local shopping malls.

I can spend hours trying on clothes at the beginning of a season or before a trip, mixing and matching pieces and seeing what works together. As my wardrobe expands each year, I have new pieces to mix with the old; my goal is always to give myself a current look with as few new pieces as possible.

Your style as a shopper and collector of wardrobe bits has a lot to do with the basics of your personality, with learned behavior, and with budgetary constraints. All of these factors change and shift, so it's natural that your shopping style will evolve over a period of years, just as your wardrobe does. Shopping style does relate to personal style because you are what you buy, but trust me, the Helter-Skelter Shopper does not look like a mess.

When you're up against it and set free in a store, what kind of shopper do you become? Take this little quiz and see if it helps to identify your shopping style.

What Kind of Shopper Are You?

1. To me, shopping is:
   A) better than sex
   B) an occupation
   C) a necessary evil
   D) a creative endeavor
2. I go shopping:
   A) whenever I can
   B) when the new clothes get to the stores
   C) only if I need something
   D) if I can find the time
3. I prefer to shop:
   A) whenever possible
   B) at lunch or on Saturdays
   C) on weekends or days off
   D) at night when stores are less crowded
4. When I find something I like:
   A) I grab it and pay; I can always return it
   B) I walk away to seriously think it over or discuss it with a loved one
   C) I try it on, then decide if I really *need* it
   D) I try it on and decide if it makes sense
5. My preferred shopping partner is:
   A) my husband, my boyfriend, my sisters, my mother, my friends—it's always a party
   B) my mom or my best friends
   C) my mom
   D) no one
6. I buy clothes to:
   A) have plenty of choices when I need them
   B) make a statement
   C) cover my figure flaws
   D) flatter and favor
7. My personal style:
   A) changes constantly
   B) reflects tasteful trends
   C) is constant and dependable
   D) is always evolving at a slow pace
8. If I have extra cash, I:
   A) hit the sale racks to load up
   B) go to Chanel
   C) save it for an emergency
   D) save it for a big style purchase
9. When I'm wearing the latest styles, I feel:
   A) sexy and sensational
   B) confident
   C) uncomfortable
   D) powerful
10. I feel "best dressed":
    A) in a new, cutting-edge outfit
    B) when I have a new piece of serious jewelry
    C) when I'm dressed in a tried-and-true winner
    D) when I have put together my own statement of style

To score, if you have mostly A answers, you are a Type A shopper, mostly B answers, Type B, and so on. Most people will fall into one of the four categories below, and while each type has its strengths and weaknesses, certain shoppers seem to enjoy a consistently higher rate of shopping satisfaction and live more happily with the choices they make—and the wardrobes that they assemble.

Type A Shopper: Helter-Skelter Give Me Shelter
Shopping Grade: C
Mistake Ratio: High
Style Grade: B+ or A
Look: Trendy and Fashionable
Suggestion: Slow down, don't waste as much.

Of all shopping styles, Ms. Helter-Skelter is the most emotional and the most likely to make mistakes. She is also the least likely to learn from past mistakes because passion is a large part of how she defines her sense of self and she refuses to deny her personal passion when she goes shopping.

"I know I make mistakes," she is thinking, "but I can't not be me."

The Type A shopper buys without trying on, buys by guessing, buys with her heart, buys navy blues to go with other navy blues and is then dismayed when they don't match. She shops with others and may even be a social shopper; she's influenced by others as well as by fads and trends and colors and store promotions. She's exciting and creative, but she'd rather own a lot of inexpensive things than any really good clothes, and her budget is often spread thin with payments on things that are already on their way out. She owns too many pairs of shoes.

Should you give the Helter-Skelter $500 of mad money for a shopping spree, she's likely to come up with a whole new look, a whole new wardrobe, and lots of cheap thrills.

Type B Shopper: The EuroSpender
Shopping Grade: B
Mistake Ratio: Low
Style Grade: B- or C
Look: Statusy, can get boring
Suggestion: Don't be afraid of cheap clothes when bought carefully.

The EuroSpender is guided by a very strong cultural bias toward buying few clothes and wearing them a lot. Her look can be either EuroTrash (lots of jewelry and very body conscious) or EuroChic (simple but safe and statusy). The EuroSpender basically doesn't like sales or markdowns or anything that could be considered inferior merchandise; she likes to buy at the beginning of the season and to put her money into one or two of the key items that fashion magazines have told her will be envied by others and mark her as one of the cognoscenti. However, she does go to "good sales" to take advantage of status merchandise at marked-down prices. She disdains these sales but goes to them anyway.

The EuroSpender doesn't want to do too much thinking or creating on her own; she feels confidence with brands; she does not take risks in her shopping methods or her personal style. This is the shopper who has brought back the luxury trade; to her, luxe was never a four-letter word. She likes cashmere, real leather, real gold, and real fur. She can walk all day in a pair of high heels, as if blisters are an affliction suffered only by other people.

Give her $500 and she buys the best-quality item she can find, from a designer or luxury-maker house at the beginning of the season.

Type C Shopper: Conservative Classic
Shopping Grade: B
Mistake Ratio: Little to none
Style Grade: B
Look: Boring
Suggestion: Loosen up, girl.

The Conservative differs from the Euro in that she doesn't care one whit about trends or new colors or what's hot—she has found her style and rarely even thinks about other looks. She gets a B as her grade because she looks good; it's just that she has no look, no real style; little of her personality shows in her choices.

Her shopping style is about going to the racks and the departments of her prechosen favorites and buying from them. She is a loyal customer to a few makers; she doesn't mix and match too much. This is the woman in the black Calvin Klein suit, the beige Talbot's pants suit.

This shopper has a more well defined signature style than most other types of shoppers although her "signature" style doesn't really make a statement about her individual personality.

Ms. Conservative is not as status conscious as other shoppers; she is not easily swayed by trends or fashion magazines. She thinks "less is more," tends to be practical and to buy good-quality clothes; she thinks fashion was made for others, not her. She is a big catalog shopper.

Give her $500 to spend and she buys a suit and a pair of pumps that she'll wear happily for a decade.

Type D Shopper: The Architect
Shopping Grade: A
Mistake Ratio: Low
Style Grade: A
Look: Smooth, elegant, not too much, not too little
Suggestion: Go to the head of the class.

The Architect is creative but she's also more careful; she is always building—her closet is her empire and the wardrobes she creates are pieces of a puzzle that are meant to work together. Architect shoppers on limited budgets know to stick with one or two color groups (most often, black), but Architects with unlimited funds still work with color groups, basing purchases on good pieces, such as shoes, handbags, coats, and other existing pieces.

The Architect also plays with texture and message—her wardrobe is flexible enough to include good-quality pieces and cheap indulgences that she melds together, often seamlessly. She builds slowly and carefully, and even if she makes a few mistakes she has enough carryover (safety net) from years of getting it right that mistakes teach her something and can either be learned from and left behind or even used to establish a new wing of her wardrobe. Her shoes are sensible but chic.

Give her $500 for a shopping spree and she carefully weighs the purchases and mixes up a cocktail of sensible and silly.

Playing It Safe

Perhaps none of the shopping types above is really *you*. There are people out there who think it's too hard to coordinate all the elements that go into making a personal statement, who want shortcuts or foolproof methods for mistake-proof dressing up. I was surprised to learn that Barbara Walters and my Aunt Lynn have the same viewpoint on dressing for success.

Barbara Walters's advice:

If you don't know what to wear, wear black.

Aunt Lynn's advice:

Wear a black Calvin Klein suit, have a really good haircut, wear gold earrings, and shake your hair so people can see the quality of the cut.

If you go by the "black is best" rule of thumb, you don't have too much shopping to do. If you only wear black Calvin Klein suits, you have even less shopping to do. Of course, by shopping, I mean the buying and coordinating and piecing together of a wardrobe. Should you opt for minimal you can make your life—and your look—easier. I think it can get boring fast, but it's an option if you have no time and/or no confidence.

The Urge to Splurge

Let's acknowledge right from the start that most shopping is done to satisfy not physical needs but rather emotional needs. Which is not to say those needs are not real. You can satisfy these needs happily with the right purchase, or make a shopping mistake if you haven't thought through what is motivating the purchase and reconciled those needs with your own style of shopping.

Most of us are forced to relate a portion of our shopping style to our wallets. We could have any sort of shopping style or personal style if there were no such thing as a limited supply of cash. I dream of walking into a store and paying full price without a second thought. I grow giddy with envy thinking of those people who can buy whatever they want, or whatever looks good on them—the suit, the shoes, *and* the bag—and do it all together as one smooth, seamless effort as opposed to having to fit together the pieces of the jigsaw puzzle that is my closet and my lifestyle.

I can barely imagine a world in which each dollar I spend is not precious or in which each decision I make is not based on what I already own, how I will use an item, and how often I will need to wear it before it "pays me back." This is the fashionistas' version of amortization—most of us are already familiar with this theory. You divide the cost of the item by the number of times you expect to wear it to get the cost per wearing and decide if you can live with that. At a certain point in its life, a garment has earned its keep and owes you nothing.

But the truth is, you can look good on any budget—the less money you have, the more discipline you have to have. Being well dressed is not about money, it's about smart choices.

Remember, in the best of all possible worlds, shopping should be a scientific endeavor; emotional shopping is what gets us all in trouble. Many shopping crimes against the budget, the body, and the mind are committed in the name of love.

All shopping arises from a perceived need, a crisis caused by a

lack or a void. (1) Eeeeek, the weatherman says snow and I have no winter coat, I better go buy one. That's real, authentic need. (2) Eeeeek, my boyfriend dumped me, I've just cut off my hair, dyed it blond, and I haven't got a thing to wear. That's emotional need based on emotional reaction.

On the other hand, there is a happy medium. I am out on a casual lark of a shopping stroll and see a black matte jersey tube skirt at Banana Republic. Something about it talks to me and I price it: $68.

Yes, my brain says, academically speaking, I can afford this skirt that ten seconds earlier I never knew I needed. Then something else happens, let's call it selective research or mode memory reflex—I remember that I own a similar skirt but that it's 100 percent wool, that I love and adore this wool skirt, that it's the mainstay of my winter wardrobe. To have a similar skirt in a lightweight fabric for summer and early fall makes great, good sense. I grab hold of the idea of duplicating success.

Note: two thought processes have happened in a matter of seconds—*price* and *need* have been surveyed and accepted. I've also done a bit of psychological dance and have given myself permission to make a purchase based on the past history of another garment. I'm hooked.

BUT Banana Republic does not have my size. Oh well.

I wander around town, poking around in several different stores, just trying to amuse myself but not really tracking the black skirt. I notice that the black tube skirt I never thought about for most of my life is very much alive and making its way into all stores. J. Crew has the same skirt. Hmmmm, this must be a trend. This must be the skirt of the season.

But wait, let's talk about the J. Crew skirt. Well, it's the same skirt stylewise, but I don't like the fabric or the stitching, so the fact that they have my size means zip. My shopping has entered another plateau. I have rejected something on the basis of quality standards.

I arrive at Ann Taylor. Voilà! Ann Taylor has the skirt, it's $75, but it's the best one I've seen. I buy it, delighted with myself.

OK, what happened to me once I spied the very first black tube skirt? A need was created. I made a scientific connection as I shopped, I edited and rejected and traded myself up in order to make a smart purchase.

Once my brain came to the conclusion that I needed a black tube skirt, I was going to have one…that day, another day, another week, another month. Need was created:

- I was attracted to the style, color, and fabric.
- I accepted the price.
- I had previously enjoyed a positive experience with a similar item.
- I became convinced that this was a trend statement for the season that would enhance my wardrobe.
- I searched the marketplace, coordinating style, fabric, price, and quality.
- I made a smart purchase.

All of these waves of consumerism and desire happened within a half hour but did not happen at one store…and at no time did I go beyond my budget or into the world of "Oh my God, what have I done?!"

The Dream vs. the Reality

Every trip to a store is made as a quest; we all dream the impossible dream. Your responsibility to yourself is to make sure you don't sell the dream short and end up in a nightmare.

Note that a lot of "need" is created in a subliminal manner, mostly through advertising and fashion magazines. Whether you tear out a photo as a real goal to attain or simply digest the material you see, you are being influenced. Need—and desire—are being established way back in the recesses of your brain.

If that need is reinforced, you will make the purchase. If your brain can override the input, you will not buy. It's that simple.

We've all heard jokes about the actor who is unable to play a role until he understands who the character is. "What's my motivation?" the actor asks. Smart shoppers understand their own cravings in order to address them better; savvy shopping often means having to figure out what's going on underneath your skin to know *why* you are attracted to a certain shopping possibility.

Most of the motivation to buy something comes from outside the store, where your personal desire is ignited by an outside force, be this advertising, street fashion, a passerby, or a fashion magazine. The concept of a look or an item enters your brain and does not sit still; the dust it causes by moving around inside your head—and maybe your heart too—is the motivation that makes you go out and buy something.

Once you enter the store, it's usually too late, unless you have taught yourself to question your every motive. If you haven't figured out where you caught the crave, you can commit an error. Once you put a name, and even a face, on the desire, you can sometimes sensibly face it down and realize that you were a woman under the influence.

Love vs. Lust

If we regret things not done rather than those we've done, then shopping regret is related to lust. We regret the items we don't buy, even though they were silly. Our heads told us they weren't worthy of us and we left these items behind in the store. But our hearts lingered on the dream.

Just as there's a "cooling-off" period before purchasing a gun, there should be an enforced waiting period before we are allowed to buy a wacky outfit or to go into debt for a fancy dress we will only wear once or before we buy a pair of shoes we know will pinch our feet. Want a navy suit? Go ahead, be my guest. Want a pink and red gauze and chiffon evening skirt on sale for a mere $168? Cooling-off period required!

The ability to walk away from an object of desire and be a smarter shopper for having done so is going to be the make-or-break point in your maturation as a serious shopper.

To distinguish between love and lust, follow these simple steps:

1. Make sure you have tried on the outfit properly as fit can be a strong enough reality check to snap you back to your senses.
2. Walk away from it, preferably for twenty-four hours or longer.
3. If the item haunts you, go back for it.
4. Try it on again. If it's still right, if your recollections of the item were confirmed, if it's *even more right* than you remembered or imagined, then yes—just do it. If doubt, even a nagging little voice of doubt, lingers under your skin, then walk away again.

If you are able to walk away and live with yourself, it was lust.

How to Shop (In One Quick Lesson)

Smart shoppers have learned how to combine these two conflicting engines—head and heart, love and lust—and come away happy, as scientific shoppers. Yet the delight in a good buy isn't coldly impersonal, as if Marie Curie had cooked up a little something for you to wear on her Bunsen burner. Few of us are comfortable in a uniform—whether an official uniform or an unofficial one. Most of us get a kick out of shopping only when we hit a home run. Yet none of us is Babe Ruth. To cut down on your chances of striking out, consider these basic rules:

Ten Rules to Shop By

1. Know your Shopping Style Type (see pages 7–14) and your Personal Style Type—these are two different things.

2. Shop alone.

3. Try it on properly.

4. Analyze your need and motivation for buying or wanting this item.

5. Unless you are out of town or running from the police, give yourself time to think about a purchase—make no thirty-second decisions.

6. Do a hasty rundown of your closet or your wardrobe for that season and consider how well this item will fit in with your existing garments . . . with your "look."

7. Will this item require additional purchases? What is the true total cost? Do you already have the shoes, the bag, the suit, the trousers, the parts, and the pieces, and will it enhance what you own or are you creating a monster? Is this item a stand-alone (see page 21)?

8. Does the quality of this item upgrade your look as a whole, keep it at the same level as your prevailing look, or actually downgrade the tone of your whole image and the other things in your wardrobe?

9. Are you taking a chance on color matches? Blacks and navy blues are particularly hard to match (see page 98) . . . if you miss the match, can you return the item? Will it go with something else?

10. Is there some correlation between the price tag and the quality of the item? Are you getting what you are actually paying for? Can you discern what you are paying for: the name, the fabric, the color . . . the what? Are you throwing away your money or are you getting many kinds of value?

Don't Do It

Never go shopping when:

- You're lonely or blue.
- You have PMS.
- You're with "the gang," and there are way too many people with way too many opinions.
- You have no money and no money coming in.

While it's true that a trip to the mall can perk up the spirits and many people vote shopping the number one cure for a bad day, there's a difference between a bad day and the kind of day when you fear even your dog doesn't love you. You cannot buy what ails you, nor can you remedy a depression with a shopping fix. You may own a new dress after the day's outing, but you're still you— with a problem. Furthermore, the likelihood of buying something to soothe yourself into "happiness" is high, and the chance for error is great. People who shop when they are seriously depressed often go over budget or buy something really dumb.

If you have PMS, your figure may be a little bloated and your mood could be a little off center—you might find that nothing looks good on you. Don't push it, just wait a few days.

The Cheese Stands Alone

What's a stand-alone purchase? Something that goes with nothing else you own and coordinates with nothing you own—in color, in style, in consistency. Let's say you have built a wardrobe of blacks, browns, grays, navy, and basically neutral shades. You fall in love with a hot-pink suit. Yeah, you could wear black or navy shoes and bag with it. Yeah, you could make it work on you . . . but it's still a stand-alone. And it should probably be left alone.

No money? Welcome to the club; most of us shop on a budget. But there's a difference between blowing a wad on something special when you have a steady income, and going out on a limb when you are flat broke, in debt, or even unemployed. Spending more in a fiscal crisis will not ease the pain. And if you don't trust yourself, simply don't go to stores. Get debt under control and then work on your shopping style so that you don't end up in this situation again.

A Final Thought

Most people can be persuaded to go shopping at the drop of a coin purse. As we approach the millennium, shopping has become a leisure-time activity—a group sport, a quick fix for whatever ails you. But this doesn't mean we're getting better at it—*au contraire*. In reality, shopping only provides the desired results when it's done with a lot of thought and planning.

Want to go shopping with the girls for entertainment? Fine, just don't bring your wallet. Never head out for a serious shopping spree without being totally prepared, without understanding that you need to coordinate the way you want to look with the way you shop for that look. Building a wardrobe—just like shopping—is serious business. Read on.

chapter 2

Manufacturing Secrets of the Garmentos

Business Before Pleasure

ok, so you want to skip this chapter.

You think you aren't very interested in manufacturing and distribution; you'd prefer that I cut to the chase…get to the good stuff. You can't imagine why I've interrupted what looked like such a promising book with such a, hmmmm, *boring* topic. You just want the shopping secrets and bargain hints.

Precisely my point.

If you want to get to the good stuff and you don't want to pay full price, or you want to evaluate full-price merchandise to see if it indeed has enough value to commandeer a chunk of your fashion budget, check out this chapter before you move to the head of the class. Secrets are *secrets* because they are hidden from the public. Few non-garmentos ever take the time to learn the things I am about to reveal; therefore, few non-garmentos know what they need to know. Get out your highlighter pen.

Business As Usual

Neither the retail nor the apparel trade has been a great business to be in during the last few years, unless you happen to be Mr. Gap or Mr. Lagerfeld. Over the last decade, though, the needs of big business have brought about many changes in the way things are done—companies have often been forced to cut corners in order to better service the bottom line and the stockholders.

There have been mergers, line extensions, and even bridge lines have been created. Factory outlets have proliferated, a zillion promotional tricks have been cooked up to get people to spend more money. Sadly, there has often been a disregard for the consumer as long as the stockholders were pleased. In short, there's been a total shift in the rules of the game so that now, more than ever, you have to know all the stages of the game in order to come out on top.

Don't expect big business to play fair.

Along with all that, take into account the surprising change in the shopping habits of the public. Purveyors of luxury goods are actually making money while middle-of-the-road and bridge line manufacturers are barely surviving. Old Faithfuls such as Sears and JCPenney have totally rebuilt in order to survive, department stores are a whole new animal than they used to be (it's called evolution), and teenagers have more disposable income than their parents, thus impacting what's sold and how it's sold.

What gives?

The answer can be found in the way that fashion is created, made, distributed, and sold. The simplified version that follows will help you better use the principles of insider shopping to divine the tricks of hidden values buried in the creation and manufacture of clothes and accessories. You should also be less dependent on labels once you find out that they often mean nothing…this will free up your shopping habits and maybe even give you more spending money and more room in your closet for smart purchases that expand wardrobe and confidence.

To beat the system, learn the system first.

Costs

Throughout the various stages of making and marketing clothes, the manufacturer is always concerned with cost and profit. This chapter deals with many tricks that can increase profits for the manufacturer. But we need to understand about basic costs.

Strictly speaking, there is a simple formula:

wholesale price − 20% = factory cost

However, if the item is imported there are shipping expenses, customs and duties, brokers and middlemen to pay off, and the equation is expected to change. Often you can travel to a foreign destination and buy the same goods for less money than in the United States simply because the cost of importing is so high.

Private-label merchandise offers the best value because the overhead costs are not as high and the savings can be passed on to the consumer. However, in most retail businesses, especially catalog and TV sales, the margin of profit (just called "the margin") is the most important part of the equation, so that limited savings, if any, are passed on to the consumer while greater earnings are passed on to the manufacturer, to the distributor, or to the middlemen. That's why it's so important to understand all aspects of manufacturing and retailing.

The Muse, Please

Fashions, styles, and trends all have to start somewhere (for more on trends, see Chapter 8). It's often said that what's old is new, but in fact fashion is not nearly that simple. Fashion is, and always has been, a very sincere statement about the times and the culture for which it is created. Fashion is living history.

If the line has a designer, the designer continually works under the very real pressure of coming up with new ideas constantly; new lines must be created at least twice a year, often four times a year, and sometimes eight times a year. The grist for the mills that will churn out salable items must be varied: reality-based and yet fantasy-edged. Where does the designer come up with his or her inspirations?

Often the designer is inspired by something in the air—usually something cultural like a movie or a museum show, but it can be as fleeting as a change in seasons or a passerby in interesting street fashion stepping from a taxi, only in view for a few seconds. Maybe it's a flea market find…or the club scene…anything may do it…that's how genius works. The vibe is out there, but only certain people have the eyes and ear to see and hear…and feel.

While designers are plugged into all these worlds, they often employ or have a relationship with one or two people who are known as professional muses—these people (most often women) have their very own sense of style and their own way of picking up vibes from the world. They spot or feel something, translate it into a perspective that works for the designer, and then pass it on.

As you may have noted year after year, the same spirits often affect a handful of designers at the same time. When that occurs, a trend or fashion direction is born. It's amazing how out of the blue, six designers will do a similar look—yet it happens all the time. When it's time for lace, everyone (who is anyone) seems to know it at the same time…even though *you* may not know it yet.

Explain how in one week of couture fashion shows, three major designers sent models dressed à la Frida Kahlo, the Mexican artist famous for her style and her eyebrows, down the catwalk. The clothes didn't look anything alike, but the models were all decked out in similar versions of Frida. When there's something in the air, there's something in the air. If two people are onto it, it's called a trendlet and bears watching. If a lot of people get it at the same time, it's a legitimate trend.

In terms of the creation of the clothes you will actually buy, there's sort of a rhythm to all this—a store in London named Voyage (say *Voy-ahge* in the French manner, please) invents a tiny little cardigan sweater in stretchy fabric with contrasting velvet ribbon trim. Said sweater costs a fortune (over $500 per), but celebrities and supermodels can afford them and *have* to have them. You think, "It's so new and creative and hot. I want it."

Such trend-spottings and manipulated cravings are regularly reported and hyped in the press—both trade press and, eventually, consumer press. Jerry Hall is photographed wearing the look, so is Meg Ryan. A buzz begins to take hold. Those who read the trade press *have* to stop by Voyage in London to have a look-see. *In Style* magazine does pages of layout with color pictures. The buzz becomes a roar. Voyage gets so outraged with the trade attention that they actually ban competing designers and store buyers from visiting their store. They issue a membership card to private customers, thus increasing the value of their little cardigans, elevating them to near-mythical status.

There's new and there's outrageous; outrageous is rarely a good investment.

Regardless, a star is born. The velvet trim thing catches on. So much so that within eighteen months, Victoria's Secret is selling Voyage look-alikes to people who don't even know what Voyage is or where it is…or care. The look is knocked off at all levels of retail and starts an international trend in velvet trims and borders.

I'm sure that when the Voyage hand-dyed and velvet-trimmed thing dies, it will die hard and all that stuff will look ridiculous, dated, and just plain silly. I will roll my eyes to think that I flew to London just to buy some sweaters there. Goodwill will be filled with Voyage and Voyage wannabes while the real Voyage will be onto a new trend, having lost nothing. That's how it goes with trends: the originator moves on and gathers no moss while the copycats are stuck looking for the next trend to knock off.

Voyage represents a specific trend. Other firms and designers create trends from classics—this is how Karl Lagerfeld re-created the Chanel empire. When Lagerfeld says tweed is "it," within a season, it is tweed. However, tweed never goes out of style, so when Lagerfeld does tweed shoes and handbags, he gives it an edge, but he isn't introducing us to something we don't already know.

Some makeup guru at two couture shows says dark raspberry lips and nails, and the world waits to see if it catches on, moving from trendlet to trend. Even though couture only has a few thousand customers, it still shakes up the world and starts trends. (For more on trendspotting, see Chapter 8.) Even when a line has no big-name designer, chances are the makers are influenced by what the trendsetters are doing or by the same influences that affect the designers themselves. Besides couture, major art exhibitions, movies, and historical statements seem to influence a whole lot of *createurs* at more or less the same time.

How Trends Become Serious Styles

In the past, it took a year for the influence of the big Paris designers to be felt in America. During this time, the over-the-top things were eliminated and the sensible ideas were shifted downgear so they could be translated into what would hopefully sell as the newest styles. Nowadays, especially with electronic information, couture can be knocked off within a matter of hours, and cheapie versions of the trends and big statements can hit the stores at the same time—even *before*–the real newsmakers' designs do.

A Galliano-designed Christian Dior gown that cost $30,000 was recently modified and copied by a moderate-priced line called ABS to sell for $200. The copy was in the stores the same season as the couture gown. No one would mistake the two, but they were of the same color (in this case, one of the most important elements of the creation), with the same style of trim and with the same feel. The intent of the inspiration was carried through to every thread of the less expensive dress.

Trends are all about selling more clothes—they make last year's clothes obsolete and this year's clothes a cause célèbre.

Couture serves many important social and financial institutions; it also serves as a barometer to what you will buy in the next year or two. Yet couture is really only a concept; it affects reality without being a concrete part of our world. Once past couture, we are into the nitty-gritty dollars and cents of making clothes and selling them to the public.

The trends lionized in couture come to the public through the fashion press and then through hype. With electronic reporting and TV coverage, the vision is instant and the world shrinks in its knowledge of design and design inspirations. Still, it takes more than just reporting the couture shows—it takes a few experts with attitude to interpret the trends, to tell you what you will and won't wear as extrapolated from these shows.

To push the envelope further, the PR people move in and offer free clothes to the visible A-list stars, especially the Hollywood set. The celebrity photos appear in magazines such as *In Style,* or video is aired on shows like *Entertainment Tonight* or on the E! cable network. Then there's a backup layer of education that comes with the hype—in-depth TV shows and articles about the designers and how they created a look or how someone should wear the look and what the look means to mankind.

Translating Style to Clothes

Everything you wear starts from a very simple equation:

trend + fabrication = price.

Most merchants will tell you that price is the tail that wags the dog; that few items move when they aren't priced properly.

Regardless of that, we as shoppers often see similar merchandise at a variety of prices, making us wonder if we're crazy or the system is too bizarre for words.

Yet each item that comes to sale is priced not to confuse you but to give away the secrets of its provenance.

Fabric: Sometimes fabric inspires the mood, sometimes vice versa. Regardless, fabric plays a far larger role in what becomes fashion than most people know or even begin to grasp. Fabric is the basis of all style and many trends.

The price of the fabric is paramount in the cost of the garment and therefore all choices a designer makes regarding a fabric must combine the fabric itself, the color, the technology, and the cost into one statement. No designer selects a fabric just because he loves it. He picks it because:

- it's not too expensive.
- it comes in the right colors.
- it comes in a width that is directly correlated to the price per yard.
- it won't require special machinery to be stitched.
- the mill can deliver the needed yardage at one time.

With all types of clothing, except couture, the cost of the fabric is taken into account because every designer and manufacturer knows the top dollar his customer will pay at retail. Very often a garment is created downward from the retail price. This downward philosophy is openly discussed or understood when the fabrics are chosen. The manufacturer has two thoughts in price: he wants to make a profit and he wants the price to be attractive to the consumer. He cannot price himself out of the market.

Also note that science and technology figure heavily into this; what can be done technically always influences what comes down the runway. War and space exploration bring new fiber technology; even the ecological movement has brought about new fabrics: polar fleece is made from garbage (well, sort of) and has been creating fashion for years now.

Fabric makers actually do a lot of the trendsetting. When a look and a fabric are tightly married, there's a lot of pressure for mills

New technology impacts fabric design. Hot designers always work with the newest fabrics; therefore, most fashion trends start with fabric.

to make cheaper versions of hot fabrics—so that velvet *devoré* (flocked velvet or velvet burn-out) was very expensive in the beginning but became available at a lower price (and lower quality) due to advances in technology.

The textures and looks science can create will indeed affect designers at all price levels and will soon be in your closet, whether you think about it or not.

Fabric lines are introduced a full year ahead of the clothing collections, so that the colors, textures, and types of materials that are going to be "in" are actually known to the trade long before the clothing hits the racks. The proliferation of certain types of fabrics and the resultant drop in price in certain categories are signs that a trend will continue—whether it's a year for denim or for velvet or for stretch lace, the trade can tell simply by how much of it is out there and at what price point.

But wait! When there's too much cheap fabric out there, and

The Fabric of Truth

Note that there is a correlation between a garment's price and quality: expensive fabric looks expensive. Yet there are three other truths:

1. Expensive fabric may not wear well.
2. Many garments or situations do not require best-quality fabrics in order to be successful. Paying gobs of money for something intended to last forever only works when the fabric is sturdy enough to give you what you are paying for.
3. New technology raises fabric prices. The cost is passed on to the consumer.

that old expression "you can see yourself coming and going" seems really true, well then, designers of higher-priced goods are disgusted and move on to new fabrics…expensive ones, technologically advanced ones, breakthrough ones. The old look dies; it makes you feel cheap even to be associated with it, and you feel an overwhelming need to clean out your closet and buy new clothes.

I paid a fortune for a high-quality Italian wool pants suit—which looks every penny of its high price tag—only to discover that the fragile wool faille snags easily and the outfit must be worn gingerly in the least stressful of situations. Also note that the converse is true—sometimes cheap fabric can fool even a sophisticated eye, and because the trend represented in the garment is ephemeral, it doesn't make sense to spring for better-quality goods.

Price: After pricing the fabric, the designer/manufacturer must price all the odds and ends that will be needed to make each garment—zippers, trim, and details all cost. If any of these has to be hand-sewn, the cost goes up, up, and up.

Throughout this text I use the example of the Voyage sweater—Voyage sweaters cost so much because they are hand-

dyed in unique colors and the velvet ribbons are sewn on individually. This sweater cannot be mass-produced (in its original format); what differentiates the real thing from a copy is this attention to production detail and cost. Oh yes, the Voyage original also has antique buttons—another costly element—and may be one-of-a-kind.

Couture commands astronomical prices because it's handmade; Savile Row tailoring is also done by hand. Items stitched by hand have a finesse that machine stitching cannot achieve; the fabric gives in to the cut better and moves with the body, molding itself in a way that machine stitching is too stiff to do. You pay for this luxury.

Even with mass manufacturing, you still pay for each and every complication: each production step, each level of quality in the raw materials, each craftsman or wage earner, and, yes, the duty for the imported bits and pieces. And you will pay again if the various trims and details require the item to be dry-cleaned (an expensive proposition) or even come apart in the dry-cleaning process, ruining the garment forever.

The more elaborate the construction of a dress, the higher the price.

Cut: After the fabric and the trims and fastenings for a garment have been selected, we move into the most cunning part—the actual pattern and sample making; this is where a technical master can score.

If the designer can change the design on a skirt in some slight way—not compromising intent, mind you—he may get twenty more skirts per hundred yards of fabric. That's money in the bank.

Because all clothing manufacturers need to show profit, they may be forced to cut corners in the making of an item, thus necessitating changes in the style, the design, or the size.

Size vs. Fit

So the designer has a pattern that works technically and stylistically. The sizes of the bust, waist, and hips, the inseam, the rise, and every other detail are coordinated by each firm. Each firm establishes its own rules for sizing, which is why you have found some makes that fit you better than others.

Certain designers also may have a concept of the build of their customer, so one sizes for a larger and fuller woman (Donna Karan) while another thinks the ideal is more straight arrow with fewer curves and less bust (Calvin Klein).

The patterns and their dimensions are called the marker. The reason that different makes of clothes fit you differently is that they all cut their markers in different ways, partly to economize and partly to flatter the figure of their ideal customer as epitomized in their fit model.

True Size

With the understanding that there are no particular "true" sizes, only some vague notions, you should also realize that you should

---

Sizing Up Fit

I was just reading an announcement in a catalog that the firm had changed its sizing and patterns, asking patrons to please use the size chart to calculate the new sizes. In catalogs it is common for there to be a body chart with actual measurements; I have no idea why dress designers don't provide the same information on a hangtag.

try on several sizes of the same garment as well as the various shaping and styling options that the manufacturer may offer.

In recent times I have worn everything from a size 8 to a size 22. I don't really know that I have a true size, but it's probably a 10-12 on the bottom and a 12-14 on the top for sleeve length. A size 14 jacket should technically be altered to fit me properly; most women should have a good alterations person on hand and learn to see themselves in a garment in relationship to the proper alterations.

All manufacturers cut their sizes differently. Try on several sizes to find your size within each brand you like.

I indicate a range of sizes because the truth is, most real bodies fall between markers: you are more likely to be an 8-10 than strictly an 8 or a 10, and so on. In couture they don't even waste time with sizes—there aren't any.

The sizes offered by any designer differ by an equal increment from each size; once the original marker is decided upon, the fit is in the cut.

Showing and Selling at Wholesale

Now we've got a line and we've priced everything and we know we can get the fabric and when we can deliver to the stores on time. Now the line is ready to be cut and sewn, but we need some sales, since we are not a charity organization and aren't in business just for the fun of it. Samples are made, but the line has not gone into production yet, since we will only produce what we sell.

Next step: sell the line to the buyers from the stores so we can know how much money is coming in and what kind of numbers we want our factories to produce.

Good houses show the clothes on live models to their most important clients; most showrooms exhibit the clothes from racks. The buyers, who represent the stores, react with all the drama of a silent film star and cut their own deals according to what they think they can sell: they love a line and want to buy; they love a line but have no more "open-to-buy" (the amount of a buyer's total budget that is not yet committed or spent for that season); they love a line, but it doesn't work with their seasonal forecast; and so on.

Finally, a deal can be struck, an order written. "I'll take that suit, but with the skirt two inches longer, and will you do it for me—and me only—in plum wool gab, please? I'll take two thousand units."

Production Values

Finally we get the line into production. (Phew!) The orders are sent to factories that will actually produce the garments. The name on the label may or may not own the factory that makes the actual clothes. Fewer and fewer firms have vertical operations.

Sample Sales

The regional salesmen of each manufacturing firm are given a set of samples of each line—they show the samples to sell the line. Then the samples are obsolete. What to do with them? Hold a sample sale and raise a little extra cash! Sample sales originally just sold samples, which were created in the no-size range between a size 6-8-10; this no-size is still referred to as "sample size." But sample sales became so successful that they became a business on their own and a way for a manufacturer to clean house and raise cash. Some sample sales are very well organized events held in auditoriums or hotels or theaters. The more bare-bones the event, the greater the profit. That means most items cannot be returned; often they cannot be tried on either. They are sold as is and may have defects.

(Do you think Ralph Lauren and Calvin Klein actually own all those factories that make their clothes? No way!)

Chances are that the clothes are contracted to a manufacturer who serves several designers and/or brands and possibly makes goods sold in a variety of price points. These guys, called "sources," are not known to the public unless something slips out in the press—like the recent mention in *W* about the fact that Sun Apparel Inc. in El Paso, Texas, makes the jeans for Ralph Lauren/Polo, Todd Oldham, and The Limited. Remember this tidbit as you read on.

One factory may make merchandise for any number of labels, from designer to department store.

Let's get back to those two thousand plum wool gab suits we ordered a few minutes ago. The contractor accepts the order. Let's say he's going to make those two thousand plum suits we just talked about. It takes 5,423 yards of fabric to make those suits. Is the contractor going to buy 5,423 yards of plum wool gabardine fabric? Don't be ridiculous, cousin. He needs at least 6,000 just to be safe and may get a better financial deal on 8,000. If he buys the 8,000 yards, he can then make an additional quantity of suits (about 750) at little additional cost or cash outlay.

The machinery keeps on running, the extra suits are made along with the designer order for two thousand units, and the contractor has, in essence, a windfall. This is good business for the contractor and good luck for the bargain shopper.

Label A (the designer's) goes into the first 2,000 plum suits and label B goes into the next 750 plum suits. They are the exact same suit, but plum A sells for $250, while plum B sells for $79. Or tuxedo A and tuxedo B come down the production line—one has a big-shot label in it and sells for $899 and the next has a no-name label in it and sells for $199.

It happens every day; it's the way of the world. The only difference in the garments, except for their labels and price tags, is

their method of distribution. The high-end suits will go to a department store; the low-end suits will end up with a jobber.

OK, academic point: there's all those legitimate labels in drawers, right? But the margin for theft of labels or hanky-panky in many areas is not small—these labels can be copied and sewn into inferior goods and sold at flea markets, or genuine labels can be hijacked and sewn into inferior goods sold at flea markets or small boutiques. Anything can happen with labels. Knowing this is reason enough for you to be frightened.

Identical garments often leave the factory to be sold at two different prices.

Better Choices Through Marketing

Now let's get back to another tangential point. If the machinery runs all day making the same product—what happens if I actively market the same product in several different ways through different divisions of my firm? Vertical retail represents each category of retail store at varying price points, so you can string them out in a vertical chart: department stores, discount stores, grocery stores. The same customer does not shop in all three, or does not

> To cover the market vertically a manufacturer may change the price and the package of its product, but it does **not** need to change the actual product.

buy the same things from all three. So a manufacturer can put the same pair of panty hose (or whatever) into a different box, call it by a different brand name, and sell it at a different price and then own the panty hose business. This means that I am developing a campaign to sell the same merchandise under different brand names without the public actually knowing the goods are identical.

Few people will ever even catch on. Happens every day. Yes, it is legal—and considered very good business practice. And that leads us to the private label business and to the store brand business. Remember our friends in El Paso, Texas, who make jeans for Todd Oldham and for The Limited? Are these the exact same jeans with different labels on 'em? Maybe, maybe not.

I can't really answer the question because I don't have two pairs of jeans in my hands. If I called Sun Apparel, they wouldn't want to tell me anything. But conceptually speaking, there's a good chance that product A and product B are identical except for their labels and the way they are marketed.

Private Label

Private label is a way by which a manufacturer produces a designer-quality item—possibly one identical to one that has a designer label—but puts a store label into it, thus reducing overhead in terms of advertising and promotion. Hopefully by reducing the overhead, department stores can pass savings on to smart shoppers.

Private label has become so important to retail that it now comes in chocolate or vanilla versions.

But let's go through the mechanics first. If the goods are the same but marketed differently, then it's marketing that accounts for the price differential. A big designer name needs to be sup-

How to Buy Wholesale—or Below

For the most part, manufacturers do not sell to the public; only store buyers can buy wholesale. They buy in bulk, and most makers have a minimum order. If there is leftover stock to get rid of, it is usually taken out of the house and dumped through a jobber, a store that sells overruns, or even a factory outlet.

As a courtesy to some members of the trade (and "the family"), manufacturers may sell a few items at the wholesale price. It most often takes an inside contact to be able to get into such a source to buy at "cost." This is not truly what it cost for the items to be made, but a technical term used within the industry. Factory cost = wholesale − 20%.

ported with fancy packaging, national (or even international) advertising, public relations, public appearances, and a whole slew of very expensive support systems.

Private label is most frequently offered by department stores. Originally it was named with the store brand (vanilla version). In recent years, however, many stores went for the chocolate version—they created their own house brand and backed it with some advertising and support. Thus JCPenney has the Arizona brand, Macy's has Charter Club, Neiman Marcus has Red River, and Saks now has several private labels, including RealClothes and The Works.

Private label is one of the best values in clothing.

chapter 3

Inside Regular Retail

The Center of Earth

the store is the center of the shopping universe: the place we go to buy the ammunition to fill our closets and our shelves. Surely there are different types of stores, offering not only a variety of merchandise but a choice in shopping styles and price strategies. But retail is a very complicated business; without understanding how it works you haven't got a shot at entering the Shopper's Hall of Fame or of getting the most bang for your buck when it comes to style and image.

Regular Retail

Regular retail is the system whereby a store offers newly manufactured goods in perfect condition at full price or what is sometimes called the "manufacturer's suggested price," which is based on the item's wholesale cost and figured at a rather precise formula.

In exchange for asking you to forgo any discounts, the store enters into a covenant with shoppers: stores provide "something for nothing," which is to say that although we pay no fee to enter, we are still provided with certain givens, including such frills as personalized service, soothing ambience, good light, gift wrap desks, clean dressing rooms, cheerful refunds and exchanges—even bathrooms with sofas and pay phones and perhaps vibrating foot massage machines. Beyond that, the store is perceived as a

member of the community, a trusted adviser, and where you go for fashion information. This is heady stuff.

Walk into the store and buy or simply browse; nothing is required of you. A regular retail store is a club for which there are no membership dues; to belong you need only relax and enjoy the privileges, soak up the information, and bask in the neon light.

Even when merchandise goes on sale at such stores and is therefore no longer being offered at full price, the system is still called "regular retail"; the services are not withdrawn. Even with a sale in progress, such a store is never called off-price or discount. The concept of regular retail is therefore related to a service and environment package as well as to price.

Regular retail stores include department stores and specialty stores, boutiques, and most of the stores in your local mall.

Department Stores

Over the past few years, department stores have had to lose some of the old-fashioned services they had for decades (no more delivery trucks), offer new services, cut stock, and replace cachet with energy, identity, and a real usefulness in order to survive.

Frankly, I think department stores have done this amazingly well. Instead of becoming dinosaurs, department stores reinvented the wheel and continue to offer the best bargains in the world under one roof. You've already read my Number One Rule of Retail (see page 7), so you know that while I don't believe in always paying full price, I do very much believe in department stores. And—hold on to your hat here—I even believe in paying full retail price under some circumstances.

Paying Full Price

There happen to be many good reasons to step back and take a hard look at regular retail and full-price shopping, to see when it does make sense. Don't look at me like that—let's hash this out. It can be smart to pay full retail when:

- You need an item in a hurry and can't waste time trying to find a similar item at less predictable (but more reasonably priced) stores.
- You must have that one, that style, that size, that fashion statement right now because of the social-cum-power messages this item will send when used properly.
  - You need alterations and your regular retailer of choice provides them for free or, at least, with ease and at a reasonable price.
  - You need the services offered, such as a personal shopper or a dedicated salesperson who knows you and your taste.
  - You rely on the liberal return policy; possibly you like to buy a lot of things and then take them home and try them on at leisure in your own home and see how they really feel

and look with what you already own, or you like to know that if something goes wrong with the garment (the color runs, it shrinks, etc.), you can return it.

- You simply can't take the stress of bargain shopping at alternative retail sources.

In some rare cases, regular retail stores do not have sales; they do not believe in marking merchandise down and *never* have sales. Honest—it's company policy. This was the policy at Giorgio in Beverly Hills, which became Fred Hayman Beverly Hills before it closed to make way for a new branch of Louis Vuitton. Not surprisingly, it is also the policy at Louis Vuitton.

Furthermore, when stores like this do have excess inventory to get rid of, they don't sell it off at an outlet store or off-pricer like most companies, *they have it destroyed!* This is a strategy for protecting their prices and image, as retail price is very much related

How to Get a Bargain at Regular Retail

Most state laws protect shoppers who pay full price by guaranteeing you the reduced price if the item you bought at regular price goes on sale within seven days of the time that you purchased it. Keep your sales receipt and head to the Customer Service desk. You need not show up with the merchandise, but you need the actual sales receipt, not what the credit card companies call the "roc"—record of charge. If you are about to buy an item at full price but are afraid it will soon go on sale, merely ask when you pay. In some cases, the item will be going on sale and you will be given the sale price, or the salesperson will hold the item for you until it is marked down. Every now and then, in order to move the piece out or reward your loyalty, a buyer will actually mark something down for you right then and there.

to how desirable an item is, and desire, as we have seen, is a matter of perception that can be manipulated.

The best way to make sure the public will pay full price for a particular item or line is to have a limited supply. The second best way is to offer service and incentives. In either case it is desire—creating a true want or perceived need within the shopper—that sells the most merchandise at regular retail and full price. *Since you now know how to distinguish real need from perceived need, take a long, hard look at your motives before you pay top dollar for a luxury item. If you're comfortable with your reasons for wanting the item and can afford it, by all means, indulge; you're likely to enjoy it for many years.*

Beating the System

Before you vow to eschew the niceties of regular retail in favor of off-pricers' more palatable price tags, it's important to grasp the financial structure of regular retail stores, so you have a better sense of what you get, what you're paying for, and where you can sacrifice or save. Once you learn the finesse in modern retail, you'll realize that in some cases it is perfectly acceptable and even smart to pay full price.

If you're about to skip over this part, remember that the whole point here is that information is power. You can't know what a bargain is until you know where the price breaks are and what kind of merchandise goes to what kind of stores and why.

How Regular Retail Works

The basic idea—from the merchant's point of view—is that the store puts up the roof, cleans the carpets and the dressing rooms, empties the litter in the ladies room, takes the risk of buying the new merchandise and the classics that you'll need in a bread-and-butter wardrobe—and the wedding gowns that only a percentage of people will need—and then lets it stand there, waiting for you to pick and choose according to your needs.

The store also provides a range of sizes, a variety of price points so that you can have what you can afford, fashion-forward information, displays that educate, and assorted promotions as quasi entertainment because people go shopping to be entertained.

These overhead expenses are reflected in the price tag; this "full retail price" includes the wholesale price of the merchandise plus a markup for the store that covers the store's expenses—as well as some profit margin. When you look at that price tag, what you should see is this equation:

wholesale price + 45% = full retail price

In business school this price system is called keystone. Some stores—usually luxury stores—do what is called "key plus 5," which means they add 5 percent to the 45 percent, making the difference an exact 50 percent. There are even stores that can build the equation so that they get 52 to 53 percent. That's capitalism.

But if you break that apart in the average, 50 percent, half the price you are paying to a store, goes for overhead and profit, so the asking price is just about double the wholesale price.

The actual cost of the item, called factory cost, is covered in Chapter 2 but, just so you can get the whole picture, is anywhere from 50 to 20 percent less than wholesale. There are many items sold for $25 that cost $8 to produce and are sold wholesale for $16. You need to understand that you are actually buying an $8 item!

Buyer's Choice

It is the store's buyer's responsibility to sell as much merchandise as possible at the full retail price, although all buyers know that some percentage will not sell and will be marked down. Still, the goal is to "sell through"—sell it all and maybe even reorder more.

Part of the buyer's job is to have a keen understanding of her customer and what her customer wants and can or will pay. Therefore, the buyer can adjust the retail price up or down a few dollars depending on what she thinks the shopper will be comfortable with. Remember this when we get to the next chapter. As a shopper you may often wonder why it is that a string of stores have the same brands and yet the prices fluctuate by a few dollars—here's your answer: buyer's choice.

Full Price on Sale

When a regular retail store goes into sale mode, the first markdown is normally 20 percent off. The second markdown is an additional 20 percent off, or a total of 40 percent off the full retail price. At the time of a second markdown, you are getting the benefits of regular retail at just about the wholesale price.

Of course, by this time, the merchandise has been on the floor for six to eight weeks, the sizes have been picked over, the condition of some of the garments may be compromised, and the trendy things must be considered a season old. Because fashion is a perishable commodity, these factors do affect price. By the end of a season, a garment isn't worth as much.

Most stores do not go beyond a second markdown because of the psychological havoc it wreaks on the foundations of regular retail; they would rather eat a loss than let you know what will happen to the clothes after they leave the floor.

This puts the pressure on you, the shopper. You know that if you don't buy at the second markdown, you probably won't get another shot at it.

Stores now get what's called "markdown money" from manufacturers, so this pays for the first markdown. Indeed, stores can still make money with after-Christmas sales if enough cash comes in and enough merchandise goes out. The store is only losing money when you get below the 40-percent-off price.

After the store has taken the second markdown, and stood its

Insider Trading Up

If you like the advantages of regular retail but can't actually afford to shop that way very often, you may consider the strategy of aligning yourself with one small store, one or two designers, or one department in a large department store where you can get personal (and regular) help from one specific salesperson who knows you, your lifestyle, your budget, and eventually, what you already own. This salesperson will also know when the clothes are going to be marked down.

I used to have a ritual whereby I walked into Bergdorf Goodman on Fifth Avenue, went to my chosen nook and cranny, and tried on the current collection of my favored designer (Louis dell Olio). I noted what fit me and in which size, as I do indeed wear a variety of sizes (see page 36). I made a copy of this list for the boutique saleswoman. It was her job to call me when the items I wanted went on sale.

This method of shopping accomplished many goals: you get many of the services of regular retail but at a savings; you have many of the services of a private shopper; you save money; and you don't have to waste time shopping. Indeed, there are many people who don't enjoy shopping around (thankfully, I personally don't know too many of 'em), and there are even more people who enjoy shopping but find they don't have the time. They also find that they make mistakes under pressure, but with a regular salesperson they save time and money as well as their image.

final ground, the sale merchandise will be taken off the floor. It is sold to jobbers who deal in what's called "retail stock"; the best example of such a store is Filene's Basement. But many department stores also have their own outlet stores now, so the merchandise can be shipped there (see pages 68–70).

How to Bargain

No one wants to be taken, and we all wonder if there's a better price to be had. Many people tell me they don't like to bargain, they don't know how to bargain, or they disdain bargaining. I love this because many of them don't realize that we *all* bargain every day in many very sophisticated ways.

Bargaining is certainly more than asking for a discount on the price of an item; bargaining is a negotiating skill that should leave both parties satisfied and may even enhance the shopping experience.

The obvious type of bargaining is haggling over price. If you aren't the kind of person who likes this sort of game, there's a very simple way to play without demeaning yourself. Simply say: "What's the best you can do on this?" or "Can you do any better on this price?"

The notion that someone quotes a price and you counter with half and you settle someplace in between is totally ridiculous. The real price you should pay in a market depends on if you are a local, if you speak the language, if you demonstrate some expertise in the art of buying the product, and if you know the going price for real people in the confines of that real world. "He paid two dollars for it; why should I pay eight dollars?" is a very good question.

Everyplace in the world overcharges in the pricing of objects to "outsiders"—in some societies the asking price is inflated several hundred percent, so that asking to cut the price in half and ultimately paying three-fourths is still an enormous overpayment. In some places the price is the price and there's maybe a 10 percent discount given to regular customers, locals, friends, family, and someone the seller takes a fancy to—but otherwise, no big change in price; take it or leave it.

But the finesse in bargaining is not in haggling over price; it's in what extras you get thrown in for the same price. Do you get a

When You Shop Is What You Pay

Part of the tradition behind regular retail is to provide full service to the customers and to have the new season's clothes in the stores in as full a range as possible very early in the season. That's why you can buy fall clothes at the end of July. There are some people, especially people who wear a large or small size, who want to buy at the beginning of the season in order to make sure they have their size and their first choice in merchandise. They are happy to pay the full retail price for this service.

The longer you wait in any given selling season, the less assurance you have of finding the styles and sizes you want, but the more the price will go down.

before the season starts = full price
eight weeks later = sale price
end of season = outlet

lower price for buying many items? Do you get a gift with your purchase? Will they deliver to your hotel or home for free? Will they ship it for free? Will they waive the tax?

A department store is a fixed market, not an open one. You can still bargain there, but it's a lot more difficult than in an open market, where the vendors survive more by wits and by the laws of the market. In an open market, they know there's give and take: they know you can take your business elsewhere if they don't give you satisfaction. Understand the marketplace and gently assert yourself to get the most for your money.

I was in a very tony designer boutique, just browsing, when the saleswoman came up to me and said, "Let me know if anything interests you. We're going to have a sale next week, but I can mark it down for you now."

Markdowns and Markups

Just about every savvy shopper knows that price tags are often come-ons, or worse, tricks. Very often items are marked up in order to be marked down.

While this is a trick we like to think happens in small no-name shops of questionable repute, the truth is that one of the most famous names in American retail is very big on this practice. This store, which I will not name, has a big catalog business and a classy branch store in just about every mall in America. This store has regular price tags on its merchandise, and the prices are high, but not outrageously high. They do fairly well.

Several times a year this store has promotional sales in which their merchandise is offered on a two-for-one basis, and shoppers go hog-wild, waxing enthusiastic over the bargains and the deals they found. The truth? This merchandise is *made* to be sold at the two-for-one price—if they attract buyers at the higher price, OK, that's nice, but the stuff is overpriced to enhance its value. My opinion? If you buy this stuff at full price, you're not a very savvy shopper.

Take a look at many promotional sales in department stores, particularly something like a Columbus Day coat sale, where stores may even boast that thousands of coats have been trucked in for this spectacular sale. Or glance across the pond to the famous Harrods sale, which is held twice a year but is most famous in January, when a celebrity is appointed grand marshal to open the doors to the public.

Both of these big sales happen to be produced theatrical events. The merchandise has been bought and created to sell at the sale price. There are few true markdowns and fewer bargains. Sure, there will be some coats that are true markdowns, and some of the merchandise at Harrods is significantly reduced, but the bulk of what's sold was created to sell at a sale price.

Private Sales

The basic rule of thumb for anyone serious about a sale is to check with the store a few days before the sale is scheduled to begin to (a) see if there is a presale sale and (b) see what will go on sale and preview the situation so you can make the most of your time. Some people even go to the store the day before and hide items and then come back and retrieve them the next day, but I don't recommend the practice—investing this much time and effort in a "bargain" defeats the purpose and is annoying to retailers.

Note that special sales and private sales often have unusual hours, so that when you are checking out the details, ask when they will open for the sale and if a line is anticipated.

In some stores, the prices just keep getting lower and lower. Ask, weigh the depth of your desire against budgetary considerations, and if the latter wins out, take your chances and wait.

Final Sales

There are times when you can return final-sale merchandise, but you have to have a damn good story and be lucky with your salesclerk. In the new tougher retail climate, I've noticed that some stores make you sign a waiver acknowledging that you have bought at a final sale and will not attempt a return.

Many Happy Returns

Returns vary in their degree of trickiness, depending on your situation. If you have the sales slip, a return should be fairly simple. However, I've noticed two rather upsetting trends of late, so you may want to check on a store's return policy before you even do business with them.

- Store credit only: More and more stores will take back your purchase but only give you a store credit, not a refund. This is particularly upsetting if you are shopping out of town or if you bought something on a whim in a store that is not one of your regular suppliers.
- Returns surcharge: This one is outrageous but may catch on—stores charge a 10 to 15 percent "restocking charge" to take back your purchase.

How to Complain

Complaining by stating what you don't like is not very rewarding...or helpful to a store. Wanting the store to guess what you have in mind as recompensation puts you both at an even bigger disadvantage. Never complain without stating exactly what you want out of the complaint. If it is not a straightforward return, explain what is wrong with the item and where it failed you.

c h a p t e r   4

Where the Buys Are—
Alternative Retail

From Off-Pricers to Factory Outlets

all forms of retail other than regular retail, with its full-price/full-service position, are called alternative retail. The public sometimes gets confused on this notion and mistakenly believes that all alternative retail offers discounted prices. This is not true. Television shopping, online shopping, and catalog shopping are facets of alternative retail, but they are also full-retail categories.

Alternative retail includes:
- discount stores
- off-price stores
- factory outlets
- consignment shops
- flea markets
- yard sales
- online shopping
- catalogs and mail order

…and just about any other type of retail, yes, even charity ball shopping.

Alternative retail is any form of selling goods other than at traditional, full-service retail. Price is not actually the defining factor here. *Believe it or not, most off-pricers (and many discounters) also make a 40 to 45 percent markup from the wholesale price.* That means television home shopping and most online shopping services are regular retail...they too are making 40 to 45 percent!

Target, Loehmann's, Kmart, Filene's Basement, and the whole slew of factory outlets that dot the landscape are considered alternative sources that can offer goods for less than regular retail yet still make their numbers because they have bought the goods for less money than what regular retailers pay for the same goods. To understand the difference between Loehmann's (an off-pricer) and Kmart (a discounter) and the kind of merchandise they sell, see page 62.

It's unlikely that Kmart and Bloomingdale's are buying from the same source anyway, but if the real question you are asking is "Is it possible that Bloomingdale's and Kmart pay a different price for the same item?" then the answer is YES, it is possible. There are reasons for this, but the reasons are related to time and stock and cash flow and even sell-through and returns.

Discount Stores

Americans love the word *discount* and tend to think there are only two types of stores in this country—department stores and discount stores. Technically, this is wrong. Discount stores are as specialized a school of thought as regular retail and, in fact, some of the best discount stores are owned by the same firms that own department stores selling at regular retail prices.

Basically speaking, a discount store offers a flat discount of 20 percent off what would be the regular retail price. My favorite discount store is Target, but there are a handful of them that are known throughout the country, including Kmart and Wal-Mart. Many factory outlet stores are also discount stores, but we'll get into that later (see page 65).

The whole point to discount shopping is that the store buys such enormous orders from manufacturers that the wholesale price is lowered to secure the order...and the savings are passed on to the shoppers. In addition, the stores do not take as large a markup as is traditionally taken by regular retailers.

Buyers and wholesalers are legally allowed to negotiate on price structure provided:

1. Prices are lowered to meet the price of the competition.
2. A lower price results in lower costs to the manufacturer because of the size of the order.
3. Goods are obsolete and must be dumped.

Discount Store Secrets

Goods can appear to be discounted—a notion that is reflected not only in the marketing of the goods but in the no-frills service of the store—when, in fact, they are selling for the price they were meant to sell for. *Yes, you the consumer are being fooled.*

Perspectives on Markup

Note that markup varies enormously, depending on where the goods were manufactured. Most things in your supermarket are American made so transportation and duties are not figured into the price. Groceries also turn over very quickly and move from the shelves. With clothing that has not been made in the United States, there's a different set of expenses.

wholesale + sea freight + customs/duties + overland freight + markup = retail

Type of Store	Traditional Markup
Department store	45–52%
Discount store	20–40%
Grocery store	3–8%

One of the ways to make more money is to create a brand that appears to be similar to a regular retail brand but sells for less money. Shoppers assume they are getting a deal when in fact they are getting exactly what they pay for.

For example, let's say that I create a product and I expect most of my sales—and profits—to come through mass market discounters such as Wal-Mart and Kmart. I know that this shopper wants to pay $14.99 for the item I'm selling. When I make the item, I create the profit margin at 45 percent and price the item to sell for $14.99 retail or $7.25 wholesale.

Working backward from the price perimeters, I create—and re-create—the item until it fits the specs and can be produced so that I can wholesale it for $7.25 and still make some profit.

So far, so good, we're all making our numbers. But I am greedy, or, uh, enterprising. I want the extra glamour and exposure of department store sales, so I sell the exact same item to department stores and so-called regular retail sources with a higher wholesale price ($9.25) and therefore a higher retail price—now the same item costs $18.99.

That extra $2 (on the wholesale price) is pure profit to me, the manufacturer. I don't expect to sell many items at this price, and I certainly don't care if they go on sale for $15.99, or even $14.99…but I have to play the game as created by the system. The system in the 1990s and into the new millennium says no margin, no dinner.

Nonetheless, the consumer has sort of been cheated. Or, at least, fooled. Today's shoppers are sophisticated enough to know that tricks like this are going on all around them—they do smell a rat—but aren't exactly sure what to do or how to detect the layers of fog blowing out from the hype machines. Indeed, unless you purchase a luxury brand, it is very hard to know what you are getting in today's market.

One of the reasons deluxe goods are doing so well right now is not only that the American economy is good and people have more money to spend but that people are confused with the way retail is stratified and they don't know who to trust aside from the very toniest brands, which rarely if ever go on sale. They pay extra money in order to feel confident about what they are getting for their hard-earned dollars.

Off-Price

Off-price is one of my favorite ways to shop because it can offer excellent savings on name brands. Off-price is what many people

mean when they use the word *discount*. The most famous off-pricer is Loehmann's, but there are many others, including Filene's Basement and T.J.Maxx, Marshall's (the same parent company as T.J.Maxx), Annie Sez, Daffy's, Ross Dress For Less, and a slew of others.

Off-price retailers buy their stock at prices below wholesale prices—often *far, far below.* The savings are passed on to the shopper, although the margins for the store can be hefty.

Most merchandise sold in off-price sources is old. It can be a few weeks older than the same merchandise that has already been in stores or it can be a season or two old. If you're looking for a classic style or a neutral basic for your core wardrobe this may not matter much; if you're looking for a trendy piece to update your look, *caveat emptor.* This is where doing your homework and boning up on what's new (and what's over) really pays off.

Likewise, it is smart to learn to recognize a designer's signature from such telltale signs as cut, detailing, and fabrics. It is not uncommon for a manufacturer to have the label taken out of a garment that is being sold through an off-price store. In the old days, Loehmann's removed the labels from the clothes they sold. This practice isn't as common as it used to be, although markings on labels or hidden in a garment are still common for inventory purposes. You cannot buy something at the Saks outlet store and return it to your local Saks for full credit because Saks marks the merchandise when it is shipped to their Off Fifth division.

Choose high-fashion items with care from off-pricers; they may be a season or more out of date.

Retail Stock

I was once chatting with a retailer friend who described the emotional upheaval that goes with buying and selling fashion—you go to a fashion show and get very excited by something you see, you go to a showroom and work with the clothes and the people and make a connection with both, then you buy, very enthusiastically.

The clothes arrive in the store and you love them and can't wait to sell them and put them on the floor with style and anticipation, and then you watch people paw over the racks and try on the clothes and buy some and leave some, and then you mark down what's left and then you see people really work the racks and the clothes get treated very badly, and in the end, whatever sorry pieces are left over get shipped out for a dollar a hanger, all your dreams broken and shattered. You try to move on, but the hurt and pain stay with you, season after season.

But wait, you ask, what happens to all those things the department stores and the boutiques can't sell? After the sales or the last call or the final markdown, where does the merchandise go to die and who gets to buy it next?

Many stores unload this merchandise to off-price stores, such as T.J.Maxx or Filene's Basement. Clothes that were once on sale at regular retail and then come to market in an alternative store are called retail stock. Sometimes they are advertised as such. Frankly, these are among my most favorite kinds of sales; I have been known to find myself in Boston on the day of such an event (you can get advance notice of the Filene's Basement sales through their newsletter) in order to do big-haul shopping.

But it needn't be a blast-off event in order to score. Some off-price stores have one rack that is marked something like "Clothing from Stores You Love"—this is their retail stock. It was from such a rack that I once bought an Alberta Ferretti dress at the Chicago Filene's Basement . . . a gorgeous, magnificent velvet and chiffon Alberta Ferretti dress, which was even in my size. This Italian designer recently opened her first boutique in London and is breaking through to international success but was at that time little known in America. Her chiffon dresses retail for thousands of dollars; I got mine for $79. Tee hee. This is a *real* bargain. I scored in this case because I had done my homework; I knew who the designer was— and the value of the dress.

The best bargains at department store sales and off-pricers go to those shoppers who recognize brands and designer names the rest of the public has never heard of.

We all have stories like this. These stories usually have happy endings because we know and understand the value of retail stock. We trust it, and we trust the advertising that supports the stores and the designers whose goods are sometimes sold like this. In fact, we often tend to trust retail stock far more than factory outlets.

Retail stock at off-pricers—and even retail warehouse sales—is often in unusual sizes, of extreme styles, or by designers who are not well known in America. If it is designer stock, it is most likely from a previous collection since most big-name design firms, especially accessories firms, base the rationale of their high prices on the fact that they offer a new style each season or each year.

No regular retail customer will pay full price for the leopard series when everyone knows that leopards are passé, finished with the last season. Out damn spots! On the other hand, those self-same leopards look more attractive in the bins of an off-pricer when they have the designer name on the tag and a marked-down price on the ticket.

Factory Outlets

Is there a more magical term in the English language than "factory outlet"? Even though I know how outlets work, I am still swayed and romanced by their lure; I once gave myself a birthday party for which I rented a bus and took my girlfriends to the nearest outlet mall. When friends come from foreign countries, the first thing I suggest to them is that we do a day at the outlets.

Needless to say, nowadays outlet shopping is a huge business, with more than three hundred outlet malls dotted around America (more in Europe, of course), and shoppers are willing to drive ninety minutes each way in order to do a day's "power shopping," during which they hope to load up on bargains for the whole family. Outlets are often located near tourist destinations (Williamsburg, Virginia; Disney World; Niagara Falls; etc.), and they usually offer entertainment for the whole family—that's everything from a comfortable place for a bored husband to sit to day care centers for toddlers. There are food courts and even sophisticated restaurants, some with their own shopping opportunities.

Factory outlets get their merchandise from many different sources and use their stores to accomplish different goals, the most important of which are:

1. to clean house of extra (i.e., unsold) stock.
2. to create brand loyalty with a shopper who cannot afford the product at full price.

There are several types of factory outlet stores, and often more than one type coexists at a single outlet center. (Note: there is also a big business in "perceived outlets"; see page 70.)

On-site Factory Stores: I sometimes call these "real" factory outlets. These stores are usually located in the factory itself or on the grounds. Once used to sell rejects, returns, and overstocks to employees only, these stores now sell directly to the public, generally at significant savings. These are the only *true* factory outlets; and they usually offer the best deal you can get. This kind of outlet is the most common form found in Europe, and although they are dying out in the United States, they still exist. The best way to find such a place is to call the headquarters of a favored brand and simply ask. Also ask about special event sales. Sometimes factories only open their doors to the public once or twice a year.

Department Store Outlets: In the old days, unsold retail stock was dumped through jobbers and off-pricers such as Filene's Basement. Traditionally speaking, unsold retail stock was sold by a store to a jobber for $1 a hanger. With losses like that, it's easy to see why the stores themselves began to have special event warehouse sales and then created their own outlet stores. At first, these outlets were freestanding and were in the boonies, so they did not conflict with regular business. Now they are most often found in outlet malls. Such stores are sometimes slightly disguised and do not carry the name of the department store they represent (for example, Off Fifth = Saks; Last Call = Neiman Marcus; The Rack = Nordstrom).

Manufacturers' Outlets: These are owned and operated by the brand itself, the manufacturer, like Ralph Lauren/Polo or Donna Karan or Nautica or even Gucci. They sell a mixture of returns, retail stock, and overruns from a single label…or from all the line extensions of a single label. But wait! There's more than meets the eye going on at these outlet stores. Such outlets may also sell merchandise created especially to sell at the outlet store in the hope of luring a new customer to the brand at a more accessible price point.

Jobbers: Jobbers aren't usually found in outlet malls, but can be—

they are stores that buy up off-price stock from a number of sources and sell them for whatever they can get. In some ways, they compete directly with factory outlets, but often they carry brands that have no other way to come to the market. Jobbers are usually community-based businesses, not national chains, and carry whatever they can get. There's a small chain in Manhattan called Odd Lot Jobbers. I pop in there every now and then because a friend once bought me a genuine Chanel silk camellia with a Chanel and Neiman Marcus tag on it for $19. You have to search a lot more at a jobber but can get lucky and be rewarded with an excellent bargain.

Fake Outlets: Obviously no outlet will admit to being a fake. My favorite examples are the ones you see in tourist destinations with signs like T-SHIRT FACTORY OUTLET. The words *factory outlet* are very seductive so people like to use them, even when they aren't accurate.

How Outlets Work

Many firms now consider the outlet business just another of their many means of distribution—a full-fledged branch of the company and a respected contributor to the bottom line.

A handful of big-name manufacturers (such as Jones New York) use the outlets to test new ideas and colors, which is an interesting form of market research. But nowadays, most firms operate outlets for profit. Rarely does a factory outlet compete with a department store because they don't offer the same merchandise.

In fact, the selection at a factory store may be far deeper than what you would ever find in a department store, because the outlet is devoted solely to all ranges of stock produced by the maker or his factories (see Chapter 2 for more on production tricks). The retail mix on the floor of any given outlet is likely to be a blend of a few current items (displayed prominently), some damaged and irregular goods, some unsold turkeys (avocado green turtlenecks), and lots of overruns. Often the damages are minimal.

Usually outlets deduct 20 to 25 percent off the so-called full retail price when they first offer their merchandise to the public. Should a department store offer you a preseason sale and deduct the same amount of money, you get the exact same price with a lot more service as well as a nearby location (outlet centers are usually located some distance from a major city, where real estate and overhead are cheaper). On the other hand, because of the mix of merchandise, the average savings at an outlet store is 20 to 30 percent. When outlets brag that they offer 70 percent savings they mean the savings off the original suggested retail price. You *can* get savings that great, but it's rare.

Manufacturers' outlets often create merchandise to be sold at a discounted price, in the exact same fashion as television shopping stations and discounters do—the big difference with the outlets is that you don't know it's not the regular line and you *assume* you've gotten the exact same merchandise that has been shipped out to regular retail stores. What is it we always say about the word *assume?* It makes an ass out of u and me!

Look at the mathematics of this. We said regular retail was wholesale + 45%. We said outlets take 20 to 25 percent off retail. So outlet price = wholesale + 25%. The manufacturer is making a 25 percent better deal than he did when he was selling to a department store, and even though he has overhead to pay, he's got plenty of profit margin. This is enough motivation for the buyers who went to Harvard Business School and the like to put their fancy MBA degrees to work and figure out more and more ways to enhance the outlet without injuring business.

Creating specialty goods for outlets is a genius concept! Furthermore, these goods are sometimes created of inferior goods with substandard workmanship, so that not only is the price you're paying less, so is the quality. Meanwhile, the MBAs in production have figured out a way to make a larger profit margin for the firm. In fact, you can bet your polo shirt that the maker has a 40 to 45 percent margin.

By manufacturing their own goods, the outlet can also have something new and fresh at the beginning of the season, in the right colors and with the cachet of current advertising programs to support it. Many people will never even notice where the garments were made or that the fabric is not imported from Italy. If you have doubts, ask the salespeople and learn how to read the labels and the hangtags; often they are coded.

If the outlet is a department store outlet, the rules are different because the department store did not manufacture the goods. Therefore, the merchandise will always be old. Don't be surprised if the item is *marked up* from the last price it had on the store floor. A third markdown does not necessarily follow the second markdown in this business. However, some outlets have what they call "sell through." This means they are determined to sell that merchandise. When it doesn't move, they mark it down, and *they keep marking it down every few weeks until it sells.*

As a general rule of thumb, outlets are a lot of fun—and especially great for a big haul at one time—but they do not always offer the ultimate bargain and may not offer any significant savings over regular retail on sale.

If you really want to score at an outlet, buy out-of-season merchandise. At the end of a season, markdowns are 50 percent; out of season, they are 70 percent.

Value-Oriented Stores

There are these enormous outlet malls that do not bill themselves as "factory outlet malls"; instead, they call themselves "value-oriented malls" or something similar. Many of the stores in these malls are factory outlets as we know them and love them; however, as many as half the stores are discounters—NOT FACTORY OUTLETS! Some of the stores may not be outlets at all.

There's nothing wrong with this, if you know what it is and what to expect—but don't *assume* that every store in a so-called factory outlet mall is indeed a factory outlet or offers any more than a 20 percent discount.

Outright Outlet Ringers

Few stores do this, but it's not uncommon, so here goes: some stores in outlet villages are not outlets, they aren't discounters, they aren't value oriented, they aren't anything except full and regular retail. By choosing to place their stores in the environment of factory outlets, they assume you will think they are outlets.

Most commonly such a store has regular retail on the street

level and retail stock, or deals, upstairs or downstairs—not on the main selling floor. Poke around, ask, compare prices.

Clearance Centers

What happens to everything that the outlets don't sell, especially if they don't work on a sell-through system? The unsold goods are trucked to one central clearance center. This is a no-frills operation, usually not in an outlet mall, and it offers really fabulous prices. Like the idea of Ralph Lauren sheets for $2.99 per? You need the sheet's clearance center outside of Atlanta.

Clearance centers are hard to find; sometimes you have to go find a factory outlet guidebook and call every outlet and ask—carefully. I usually do this by playing a little bit stupid, since I find this is a good way to get information that might not be forthcoming if you just asked for it outright. Try this gambit:

"I bought a suit at the outlet and now that I've worn it so many times and I love it, I realize that I should have bought the pants that go with it. I went back to the outlet but they don't have these clothes on the floor anymore. Is there a place where you send all the leftovers so that I can call and track down the trousers and see if they have my size?"

Used Clothing

If you crave designer and bridge lines but haven't got the patience for outlets, consider resale and consignment shops.

At one time fashionable ladies gave their outdated clothes to friends, maids, or charities. Since the recession years in the 1980s, however, more and more women decided they should raise a little cash when they dumped their "old" clothes. Now these clothes are often sold to very fancy resale shops so that madame may recoup some expenses to advance her next shopping spree.

Most of the world's big shopping capitals have fancy resale

Your best chance of a consignment store score is in a wealthy zip code.

shops where gently worn (this means used) clothes are sold for about half what they cost new. They are meant to be of a current style and therefore not vintage; most stores refuse clothes that are more than one year old.

The basic idea is that someone else wore these clothes for a season until they were, egads, a year old, after which such a person couldn't be caught dead in them. Some of these garments may only have been worn by models on the catwalk or for photography

Cinderella Time

I have very large feet and lots of trouble finding shoes . . . I wear a size 10½ or 11B. I do have a secret source, however: a local consignment shop where there is a consignee (#0024) who has sort of the same size foot I do—she leaves behind mostly size 10½ shoes, but every now and then a size 11.

Here's the great part:

• She's already broken in the shoes for me.
• She has great taste and buys good stuff—everything from Manolo Blahnik to Bally to Ferragamo and beyond.
• She must be very well off because there are often a lot of different styles in the same colors and many of the shoes are barely worn.
• The asking price on a pair of her shoes is $55 to $65.
• The shop has half-price sales, so I have often gotten shoes for $20 a pair.

If you can find a local sole mate (excuse the pun), let the store know you've found a good match and ask them to call you when that consignee brings in her goods.

Also note that sizes—especially shoe sizes—change with wear, so when you go to a resale shop, be sure to try on a range of sizes.

shoots; some have gotten less wear than that, as they hung in the closets of women with so much to choose from that they just never got around to wearing the items very often—if at all. This means that some used clothes are actually new.

The stores that sell them fall into three different types: very selective stores that only sell big-time designer names; stores that sell designer and designer bridge lines; and stores that sell whatever they get, which is the category that most thrift shops and charity shops fall into. The first two types are usually consignment shops.

Get Thee to a Consignment Desk

Curious about the whole process, I took an armload of items to the fanciest consignment shop in New York. Their stated rule is that they do not accept items more than two years old, but I observed a helluva lot of Adolfo suits and Mr. Adolfo had been out of business for more than two years when I tried my excellent adventure.

The store had a back door for wannabe consignees to which I was directed; I was then asked to wait until someone came to look at my things. I waited almost a half hour. The woman who eventually came to help me was not friendly. I explained that my sister had just died and that I had cleaned her closet and had a mixture of things to dispose of, including several Adolfo suits like those I had seen in the front room.

My hostess sneered at the Adolfo suits, saying their age made them ineligible for consignment. Though she did deign to offer a pittance for a few items, including a Judith Leiber handbag, which was unused and still in its box that she thought she could sell for $125; I would get half of that. Knowing that the bag had retailed for $500, I decided she could keep her $62. I found the whole experience so unpleasant I have never tried to consign anything since then. I would much rather give it to charity.

Consignment shops have become especially popular and can be found in not only big cities but also well-heeled suburbs. There used to be just a few very fancy consignment shops where very public figures and wealthy matrons sent their clothes—two in New York made their reputations on the rumor that Jacqueline Onassis sent her things there. Now these shops can be found in any upper-middle-class neighborhood of America.

Used clothing has usually been dry-cleaned before it is put on the racks, although it is still important to check for stains, odors, and stress wear. If it is being sold "as is" look to see what the flaw is—if it's missing a button or has a small hole or tear.

The best used clothing stores are in cities (and suburbs) where rich people live. The best *bargains* are in stores in less affluent cities where you luck into something good, or in affluent cities where the salesclerks don't know what the labels mean when they sort the merchandise.

For example, I lucked into a Laura Biagiotti cashmere and silk sweater at my local Goodwill store for $25. Laura Biagiotti is a very famous Italian designer who is not well known in America. Although my local Goodwill store does have a "boutique" area where the more expensive clothes are sold, this sweater was mixed in with the general sweater population—obviously no one knew what it was worth (about $350).

Tag-sale prices may be the same as retail prices—but the tag-sale goodies are used. Watch out!

Tag Sales

In the part of the country where I live, they are called tag sales. Elsewhere they are garage sales or yard sales—all refer to those sales where a homeowner decides to clean house and sell all the items he or she no longer wants. When

Five Things to Buy at a Tag Sale

1. kids' clothes
2. dress-up accessories
3. sunglasses
4. artificial flowers
5. uniforms, surplus classics

such a sale is held after a death in the family it may or may not be called an estate sale.

Clothing is featured at many of these sales.

A tag sale is one of your best chances to get a good bargain because very often the seller does not know what he's selling...or care. I once bought Chanel earrings (not only real Chanel earrings but with the Chanel boxes and the tags on them) for $10 a pair—the woman said she knew what they were but she just wanted to get rid of them. OK—no problem!

Sometimes tag sales are managed by professionals, who convince homeowners that they have a buried fortune lying around and should turn over the stress of the sale to the pros who really know the right prices and therefore command higher (and more fair) prices. This is an excellent marketing ploy. Mostly I find that these pros don't know their stuff very well—they just think they do—and can even price some items higher than their original retail prices or well beyond a competitive market price. Be careful!

And do remember some bargaining is expected at tag sales, especially if you buy a lot.

Flea Markets

Most flea markets sell used or vintage clothing and what the trade calls "smalls"—small decorative items that you can carry with you. Some do sell large pieces of furniture, and some types of markets do sell new items. The most difficult to buy are these new items because layers of tricks can be hidden behind the prices.

Flea market shoppers *assume* that prices must be low because, hey, it's a flea market. The merchant has no overhead, no staff, no dressing room. In fact, prices are often equal to regular retail or even higher! Furthermore, the goods may be seconds, irregulars, overruns, or even fakes. To disguise this fact the vendor will price the goods at very close to the regular retail price so the shopper does not smell a rat. Wake up and smell.

Vintage Clothing

There is a difference between vintage clothing and used clothing, although the older you get, the more you wince when you find out that half the clothes you gave to Goodwill are being touted as the latest collectible in vintage wear.

Vintage clothing is as much a state of mind and style as it is a definition or date of manufacture. Vintage clothing is clothing from a specific style in the history of fashion—it must make a

Five Smart Vintage Buys

1. anything not in style
2. jewelry that's funky
3. men's ties
4. blue jeans
5. slips and lingerie looks

fashion statement to have any value. In most cases, the style has gone out of fashion and been forgotten, then is rediscovered by an underground movement of kids or clubbers that spreads it to the mainstream. If it really catches on, new versions of this old look will appear in reproduction form as well as in adaptive form.

The best barometer that your thrift store find is vintage fashion is that you pay $5 for it and your mother hates it. Your friends think you are nuts. Or all of your friends think you are nuts, save one…who really, really gets it.

I knew a young woman back in the sixties who dressed herself only in flowered housedresses she bought at the Rose Bowl swap meet in Pasadena, California. She spent about $5 each for these little numbers, which everyone else made fun of, and was considered so chic and cutting-edge that *Mademoiselle* magazine did a feature on her and *Women's Wear Daily* brought her to New York to be a fashion editor. Honest.

This woman used a specific vintage look to express her personal style. When trends are inspired by vintage clothing, they invariably start in the same way and move from ugly and unacceptable to trendy, must-have gear. Of course, much vintage just serves a need and never gets to the trendy stage.

Many years ago I fell in love with those plastic beads from the

1950s—not pop beads—strands of colored chunky beads, often in garish colors, that can only be called *mouche,* as the French would say, tacky or ugly. Certainly kitschy. I would buy them at tag sales and flea markets, usually for no more than $1 to $3 per necklace, though I have paid as much as $20 under certain conditions.

If you frequent flea markets and vintage clothing shops, you probably fit in one of these categories:

- You have no money, don't care about current styles, and just latch onto something that speaks to you in a flea market or vintage source—this is how the retro seventies look took hold.
- You have a specific need for a certain event, no budget for new clothes, and decide on a vintage version of the appropriate gear that will be whimsical yet socially acceptable . . . say an old tuxedo jacket or prom dress from the sixties.
- You enjoy making an antifashion or even antisocial statement.
- You are trying to achieve a current look by going back to the original inspiration. For example, a few years ago couture suddenly started to show beaded chiffon dresses, thin, slim, chic, and slightly flapperlike. At a tag sale, I found an original of such a dress for $5. It smelled slightly of mildew and age and old perfume but the colors were sublime. I wore it once, copying a total John Galliano look that I had seen in a fashion magazine. As I was dressing for dinner the dress began to fall apart—I wore it through the evening, loved wearing it, then threw it out that night. (Sure makes packing easier.) Many fashion inspirations are derived from vintage clothing. Sometimes the original is cheaper than the couture version.
- You have already seen other people wearing a style and you want in on the action before it goes mainstream.
- You have seen others wearing a certain style and it sparks within you another idea that you then begin to style.
- For fashion or nostalgia reasons, you buy and collect from specific eras, styles, or designers. I suddenly got a yen for Pucci at a time

when Pucci was not even on the cutting edge of a return. I found a velvet skirt (it almost even fit me) in Rome for $50 and bought it, fulfilling my need for Pucci. A year later, Pucci became the hot collectible in the chichi international fashion maven club. I felt no need to continue to add to my collection, especially when I saw that prices were in the $200 to $400 range, so I moved on.

How to Buy Vintage

Vintage clothing stores are more and more popular and have stratified, so that there are Army-Navy type stores in America that sell used clothing and some vintage, vintage stores that specialize in certain decades or styles, as well as high-end vintage clothing stores where designers hang out and collectors buy items they consider important works of art.

When you're buying vintage, the first question you need to ask yourself is if you are buying the item to wear it or not.

Here is a checklist of things to look for and realities to take into consideration when you're buying vintage:

- Condition is the primary concern with any collectible item. The more expensive the item, the more important it is as a collectible or statement of time and place, the more critical that it be in mint condition or as close to it as possible.
- Check for wear at stress points—look at seams inside and out. Look at the actual construction of the garment or item. If it's a handbag that you plan to use, operate the clasp and check that its current condition can absorb the stress of modern use.
- If the item is silk, pull on it gently to simulate stress to see if it's about ready to shred.
- Check for spots and stains, then figure out which ones can be expected to clean up and which ones are there for good and decide if you can live with that.
- Smell the item and understand that natural fibers will release stains

and odors better than synthetics or blends. Be especially wary of mildew. Mildew grows and needs to be killed before it destroys an item.

- Understand that the older a garment is, the less well it will adapt to modern living—you can't do a whole day's work in a vintage piece (wear vintage items four to six hours at a time, max).
- Don't put vintage clothing in the washing machine—do baby it and find a dry cleaner who understands what the item is or provide your own TLC.
- Consider making some modern revisions to help your garment live and breathe longer—sew in grosgrain ribbon at the waist; wear a slip underneath or even another dress.
- Understand that by wearing a vintage item you are hastening its death. You may get only a handful of wearings from a vintage piece before it gives up the ghost for good.

Catalogs

My definition of a great evening is to take a hot bath in sweet-smelling scent, pull on comfy pajamas, and sit in bed and thumb through catalogs. Catalog shopping brings all the joys of window-shopping right into your home and many of the practical aspects of easy shopping to your home phone.

As long as you understand that catalogs do not usually offer a bargain, and the price you pay for shipping and handling can be outrageous, then you're set. Sometimes the convenience is worth the extra cost.

There are several types of catalogs; each type reflects the same differences that are available in stores. All department stores have a catalog business and possibly a catalog business with many divisions, such as the one operated by Saks Fifth Avenue. Saks has a separate catalog division that sells clothes that are sold in the stores and another that sells clothes that are *not* in the stores!

Obviously there are plenty of catalogs that sell their own

vision, their own concepts, and their own merchandise that cannot be found in regular retail stores because it is made for them. Then there are catalogs that sell a look; this look is created from merchandise that can be found in many other sources, but it has been edited to a uniform.

There are brand catalogs, there are discount catalogs, there are lifestyle catalogs, and there are bread-and-butter catalogs. It's a huge business. So large, in fact, that there are even stores that specialize in selling off-price goods that come from catalog sources and resources (find a Steinmart store). Catalogs are a lot of fun and a very convenient way to shop—but there are a few things that you should remember:

- Catalogs usually get the full 40 to 50 percent markup on their goods—there are few bargains.
- Prices on the same goods can be different in the same catalog—firms experiment with prices and regional tastes by sending different versions of the same catalog to different zip codes. More affluent zip codes often have higher prices.
- Tax, handling, and shipping charges can add significantly to your outlay—although not all states or firms charge tax. Ask and try to avoid tax.
- Items, especially garments, may not look like they do in the pages of the catalog when you have them at home. Colors don't reproduce well on paper, and fit can be altered on a model. Also photography is an art—even a lousy garment can look like a million bucks when photographed properly.
- Fit is variable to the maker; use the charts provided and assume nothing. What size you are in "real life" may be meaningless to a certain maker's size and fit program.

- The switchboard operator at a catalog firm has been coached in the art of the "upsell"—once you're on the phone with your order, you may be talked into buying other items or even offered special promotions that are not in the catalog.
- Many catalogs operate retail stores that sell the exact same merchandise for less—shop in person and you'll certainly save shipping and handling costs and you may even find the merchandise you want marked down.
- While most catalogs allow you to make returns, you must pay for the postage on these returns yourself and police your bills to make sure the credit has been recorded.
- Catalogs do have sales and their own factory outlets; ask before you finalize your order if the item(s) you want have been (or are about to be) reduced.

Television Shopping

Before I talk too much about TV shopping, you should know that I do work with QVC—I may have a bias in their favor, but I also have an insider's view.

Television shopping has grown a lot in the last ten years and will become more and more sophisticated in the next decade. People like to think that TV shows offer incredible bargains, but they don't really know how the system works.

TV shopping offers you a better price because the manufacturer discounts directly to the TV network.

TV retail works just like regular retail—if there is a price break on the goods, it's not because the TV network is taking a smaller markup as a discounter might. More often, the networks function more like an off-pricer—they get a better wholesale cost because the maker very much wants to sell to them.

The TV networks do not have warehouses and storage space for merchandise, so the items they sell must rotate in and out at a rapid pace. Therefore they order a lower quantity than what they think they can sell and hope to sell out as quickly as possible. After an item has been featured, its sales figures will tell the computer a number of important marketing factors so that when the TV networks want to sell that item or that type of item again, they will know how many they sold to what part of the country and at what time of the day.

The best deal for the TV networks is merchandise that is not sold in stores—this exclusive pitch makes the viewer at home more likely to feel the need to buy immediately. Furthermore, if the item is backed by a celebrity, it will probably sell even better. Therefore most of the celebrity-oriented merchandise you see on TV has been created as a private label business for that star.

(For the lowdown on how private label works, see pages 49–50.)

People like Richard Simmons, Victoria Principal, Tova Borgnine, and Joan Rivers have made a fortune selling products on TV because they can control the manufacturing costs. The TV networks do not pay these people to appear on the shows; they instead get a percentage of the sales. In many cases, they get a percent from the TV networks and the manufacturer.

The other way that TV networks get good prices is through selling excess retail stock, just as off-pricers do. A perfume company has five thousand Christmas gift sets left over in the warehouse. Christmas is long gone, and they can't sell them at retail. They are paying to warehouse these sets, and the sets are worthless. They can dump them at a factory outlet or through a jobber, but five thousand isn't a lot of stock for a venture like that. Better, they invest fifty cents per unit, repackage the sets in a pretty basket, and sell them at a slightly discounted bulk wholesale price to a TV network, which will now have an exclusive for its viewers. Win-win, huh?

Mostly, TV networks get their goods from the same big-time, big-name firms that sell to department stores and other stores you know and trust. But department stores can only sell so many thousands of units of any given item. TV can actually sell a million units of one item. In order to have the opportunity to sell their goods on TV, and with visions of large sales figures dancing in their heads, these manufacturers lower the wholesale price to the TV network, and the network passes these savings on to the consumer.

chapter 5

Putting It All Together—
Building a Wardrobe

The Building Block Theory

now that you understand the basics of manufacturing and retail sales, you're ready to go shopping. With any luck at all, you'll be a more savvy shopper, more in tune with the possibilities behind a label and what the sale cycles are in terms of markdowns at your favorite department stores. But don't just dash out there and buy indiscriminately—have a plan so that everything you buy fits into the whole of your personal look and creates more confidence.

A wardrobe is built in three stages:

1. The Empty Stage . . . Help! I have nothing to wear!
2. The One Good Stage . . . in which you invest in one good example of each category of needs—one good coat, one good belt, one good handbag, one Little Black Dress, etc.
3. The Rounding-Out Stage . . . in which you fill in with assorted pieces and accessories to update each season and give greater consideration to trends while continuing to upgrade and refine your overall look.

Don't think that once you've reached stage 3 all you'll ever need to buy again is a trendy new scarf now and then. Very few people go through life unchanged, or even in the same direction, so that wardrobe is a living, breathing organism that needs to be treated as such. The stages repeat themselves throughout your life, especially at life changes (new jobs, new locations, new challenges at work, children, social changes, etc.). As you roll and pitch with life forces, be mindful of the three stages in order to avoid waking up one day with truly nothing to wear . . . or having to go into serious debt just to dress properly. I've noticed that people who set out to create an instant wardrobe almost always make shopping mistakes and often go into debt—sometimes serious debt.

Defining Your Look

Because what you look like says so much about you, it's important that you use the pieces of your wardrobe to convey the message you want the world to receive. This is where Personal Style comes in. Personal Style should sum up who you are in all facets of your life— you may be a flannel granny gown person or a black stretch lace negligee person . . . yet you may still wear a black or navy suit to work. Style is made up of layers because style is an aspect of personality and confidence.

Your Personal Style melds your lifestyle, finances, and identity into an overall fashion statement that makes you feel good about yourself and tells the world how to feel about you.

Having Personal Style is having the ability to present yourself appropriately in any endeavor and to look right for the occasion while still showing some sense of your personality. We'd live in an episode of *The Twilight Zone* if we all wore the same things.

I hate these categories of "looks" that are often in magazines and books—you're Preppy, you're Traditional, you're Hollywood. I think most of us can be anything; we have parts and pieces of many looks within our souls and are most often forced to express a look that frequently does not represent our own personalities, thus compelling us to create a hodgepodge look made of compromises and prayers. It doesn't really matter how Cowboy you are in your heart, if you work for IBM you aren't Cowboy from nine to six.

The reason it's so hard to find a look that we like—and makes us feel good—is that a look must please us and our immediate world around us, yet sometimes we are in a hostile or difficult environment. Having to do all this on a budget makes it that much harder.

Everything you buy should be part of the whole, and each piece should move the whole image forward into the next season, the next meeting, the next job.

Finding a New Personal Style

If you aren't happy about the image you think you project, before you go out to buy new clothes, spend some time visualizing what you would look like and the kind of clothes you would wear if you could burn your entire wardrobe and start from scratch. Then begin to develop your new Personal Style from magazine cuttings.

1. Leaf through every fashion magazine you can find and tear two different kinds of looks from advertising and editorials—those that you think represent what you look like now (or the kinds of clothes you buy now) and those that represent what you wish you'd look like.

2. Start two file folders (OLD and NEW) and add the pages into the files over a period of several weeks, even a few months.

3. At a time when you're well rested and at your best, examine the two files with a pencil and pad at hand.

4. Now look in the NEW file and do a final discard search. Throw out the stuff that's just a dream and doesn't really work; get the pile down to a serious wish list.

5. List the overall elements of style in your wanna-be look and then list what specific purchases you should make to get there.

6. At the same time, list those elements that you want eliminated from your current look.

7. Keep the lists with you so that each time you go shopping, you can overcome your original inclinations and shopping styles and begin to guide yourself toward the dream goal. The new look isn't about money, it's about discipline—you can figure out how to look that way on just about any budget.

Signature Style

Few young women have a signature style; this is something that comes as we get older and have experimented for years. It's also easier to start with a "signature statement" rather than a complete and total signature style that can box you into a corner. For example, I am known for my armful of bangle bracelets and for wearing two watches. I don't wear them every day, but I do wear them when I'm "out" and dressed up. Very often a signature statement helps you define your overall style without confining you to an inflexible look.

Sally Jessy Raphael is known for her red Lucite eyeglass frames; Carrie Donovan for her large, round black frames. I know a man who only wears polka-dot ties. A poet named Marianne Moore only wore tricornered hats. Accessories are a good beginning for a signature style item.

Ways to create a signature style:

- Wear only one color.
- Wear the same signature items every day.
- Make overall statements that educate your friends and family: "Oh, I love that, but I only wear black these days—it's so clean."
- Don't get bored with the statement after six months; this confuses your public.

The Bottom Line

No matter what your style, all your energy should be directed toward one simple goal: creating a look that puts you at ease so you can face your days (and nights) without fretting over the fashion parts. I've found that how I *feel* in the clothes is as important to me as the clothes themselves—maybe even more so. I want to sail out my door looking like a queen and feeling the power that confidence gives me. I want my clothes to convey a silent message to all who gaze on me that both reflects my professional competence and hints at some parts of my personality.

Getting the looks part out of the way allows you to get down to business and the true priorities of your life.

That's not to say that I always look perfect—or even look good—or that I leave the house in a costume. You're as likely to find me slinking around the Stop & Shop in jeans and a wrinkly sweater as you are to notice me dressed to the teeth in an important designer suit. In fact, I consider both looks to be the real me and an important part of who I am.

The point of it all, therefore, is to know yourself and your needs and your objectives as a woman and in business and in the whole of your lifestyle. Then you can synthesize the clothes out there in the marketplace and eliminate the "in" stuff or the merely kooky stuff that looks really attractive on a model on a glossy page but is a big mistake in real life; then you can look at your checkbook and the offerings in the stores and reconcile the two and come out ahead; then you can grasp the pieces offered to you from the smorgasbord of retail and perfect past mistakes, hone current nuances, and come out proud of yourself.

It's all a matter of making the right choices.

European Philosophy

I'd first realized that French women had a different style from Americans on my first trip to Europe, when I was nineteen and desperately trying to pretend I wasn't traveling with *them* (my younger brother and sister). To me, European women seemed to wear only black and white and to wear the same clothes constantly as if it were a uniform: black skirt, white blouse. Not even a circle pin!

I, on the other hand, was wearing an orange voile dress printed with giant flowers à la Carnaby Street and thought the French girls were bor-rrring. In my mind it was a triumphant fashion year for me, sort of my coming out, and I was incredibly hot and hip. It took me years to figure out how smart they were. The moral of the story is rather simple: don't wear orange voile when you could be chic. Wear orange voile when you don't know any better.

If you've been to Europe lately, you may have been astonished by the high prices; you'll also find the cost-of-living index far beyond American standards. People's salaries are lower, and prices for everything from food to clothes are much higher. Furthermore, you'll find a retail structure that supports the cost of living and keeps it high—there are few cheaply made goods imported for the sole purpose of selling them cheaply. The notion of "cheap thrills" does not translate into any foreign language I know.

The European shopper, since she has less money in her pocket, spends it on fewer garments and must choose them with care. The European woman buys well-made classics and wears the hell out of them.

She does this in two totally different ways that complement each other— she buys classics that will last forever, and then she fills in with a few good pieces in the color of the moment.

1) Classics
European women depend on the bare bones of structure and classic style because few have the extra money to be frivolous. Madame might buy a tight

little leopard-print miniskirt or a stretch-lace spandex slip skirt in the dime store for a kick, but she will not buy trendy fashion or dime-store clothes for everyday wear. Even if she can afford only one good item per season, she will buy the very best she can manage, saving up and reaching out for it rather than making do with lower quality or a lesser brand.

Brand is important in this equation, but it's not the answer to everything, because since childhood our European model has been trained to spot look-alikes that are almost as good as what the big-name houses offer, but cost less. Fooling Mother Nature, or at least the Joneses next door, has been a hobby of many mothers and daughters for generations, and much time, effort, and education have been spent to get the very best for the least amount of money.

What has supported the old "black skirt and white blouse" theory was the idea that the women supposedly could afford only one high-quality black skirt and one or two blouses, and so they wore them to death, dressing them up with accessories. I have a feeling that this idea grew out of B movies from World War II or from postwar stories from time period when people were lucky to be alive, let alone chic. So the black skirt–white blouse concept is actually a stereotype that makes a point, but the philosophy is hardcore: less is more.

2) Fashion-Forward Color

In Europe, color trends are far more important than in America and are taken very seriously. The European woman jumps on these fashion-forward shades to complete her wardrobe and her seasonal statement about herself.

At the beginning of a trend, only the best design houses have those shades that are decreed to be "in." Wearing the color of the moment indicates to the European world that madame knows what's what and who is who. She will not buy many items in this color, but she will buy a few and will team them with her basics and classics. This sends the signal to her peer group that she is plugged in, which is very important in the closed societies of old Europe. This also sends a signal to mass marketers in fashion, as the "in" color in Milan one season will probably be the "in" color in New York's better dresses the next season and in moderate dresses and low-end clothing the following season . . . but only if the color has legs and walks out of stores on its own.

So European women, in buying the proposed color of the moment, dictate whether or not it will define a time. Coral had a short reign of terror, whereas apple green has survived more than four years of scrutiny. Ice blue is just emerging. Gray flannel is worth ignoring.

How expensive and how hot the individual items bought in the new "in" shade are will better define madame's status to her world. For the most part, these color goods are meant to be worn only a season and then are moved to the back of the closet or discarded (taken to a resale shop). Only a few colors beyond the classics of navy, gray, brown, burgundy, red, and black will have the staying power to last several seasons, and fewer still will become classics.

European women will be very big on mixing the color of the moment with black. This is also done in the United States, but not nearly to the same degree as in Europe. For some reason, the color of the moment is rarely mixed with navy, gray, or brown—in Europe or in America. In fact, these basics aren't nearly as basic to the European philosophy as basic black. Despite projections that chocolate is the new black, that gray is back, or that pink is the navy blue of India, European women stick to black plus color, or black plus white or cream.

For the European woman who cannot afford to go overboard with trendy colors but who still needs her fix, fashion-forward accessories are artfully used. They will range from dime-store looks, also meant to be disposable, to luxury goods—such as the Hermès scarf of the moment, which invariably reflects the Hermès theme of the year.

Combining cheap accessories and weird shades is tricky, of course, since no one wants to go too trendy and be stuck with something—especially something expensive—that won't go the distance, so the philosophy of jumping on the bandwagon must be treated with a jaundiced eye. Style may be forever, but fashion is not, nor are themed accessories or dating gestures of extravagance or indulgence.

The woman who buys the hot themed item is invariably going to give it away or sell it at the end of the season or the year. If it's very fashion forward and of good quality she may unload it at a resale shop.

Wardrobe Building Blocks

Knowing your budget and the ratio of budget to each category of clothing you are about to buy is an important step in conquering fashion errors. You may well find a fabulous anything at a good price, but it doesn't extend your wardrobe in an equation that justifies laying out the cash.

The power base of any wardrobe is its versatility.

The underlying factor in good wardrobe buying is the understanding that this is a living, breathing, changing creature and you never want to be in the position of having to start from scratch. While few women over the age of thirty have elements of their first wardrobe in use today, the process of renewal is meant to be a gradual one with a few pieces added and retired each year.

Allocate your budget so as to give your wardrobe the most flexibility where you need it, which, for most people, is in everyday clothes (not evening gowns!). If need be, create for yourself a simple chart with an equation of the ratio of your time spent in each pursuit that constitutes your whole life. What percentage of your time is spent in work clothes, in casual clothes, in exercise clothes,

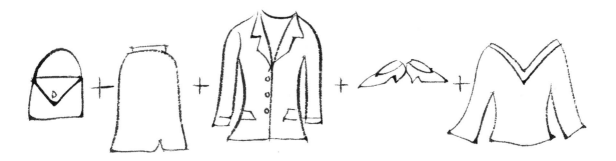

in black-tie clothing? These percentages should tell you where your disposable income should be spent.

The Balanced Pie

If you're the kind of shopper who is easily swayed by what's in the store—especially if it's on sale—then perhaps you need to be reminded of what's in your closet or where your own "open-to-buy" is located. *Open to buy* is a trade term that store buyers use; it refers to the amount of money left in a budget in any given season that can be allocated to whatever they pick. From the pie graph that represents your wardrobe as a whole, you have to keep track of how to best maintain the balance. The best way to do this is to know what kind of clothes you need most.

Always attempt to maintain a balance in the whole of what you own.

Review the list below, then use these and/or other categories to fill in the chart at the back of the book (see a sample on page 96.) to get a hard look at your own reality. Are your clothes paying for themselves, or do you have too much money and wardrobe space tied up in dressy clothes or shoes and accessories when you should have a bigger selection of work clothes?

Clothing Categories

High-powered suits
Matched business suits
Casual business suits
Skirt and sweater ensembles
Blouse (white or cream)
Blouse (solid color)
Blouse (print)
Sweater
Twin set
Stand-alone skirt
Stand-alone trousers
Stand-alone blazer
Casual outfits
Little Black Dress
Non-black party dress
Evening gown
Ball gown
Evening trouser suit

Item/qty		Times Worn		
		per week	per month	per year
black trousers	2	at least 1	4/6	48-72
cream turtleneck	1		2/3	24-36

Once you've filled in the chart, it should become obvious where to spend most of your shopping dollars and where to cut.

The breadth of any given wardrobe is very much related to your age, your financial status, your job and its requirements, your devotion to dress-down Fridays, and how you spend your leisure time. Parenthood also affects choices, as does physical body type and even the part of the country you live in.

Naturally you want to also reflect who you are as a person. This is a lot more tricky because in many arenas in corporate America, management doesn't want to know who you are as a person and doesn't want you to look too different from anyone else on the team. Artists are allowed to look/dress creatively—it's expected and accepted. Lawyers do not have this freedom, although lawyers use their wardrobe to manipulate just the same. Every smart businessperson uses her clothing to send a message to the viewing public—a message of power, of vulnerability, of creativity, of purity, as the case may be on any given day.

Nothing in your closet should get there by accident; everything you own and wear should be put on your back for two reasons only, and the right outfit fulfills both needs:

- to convey a message to the viewer
- to make you feel good about yourself

Start-up Wardrobe

At each of life's major junctions there's a need for a new wardrobe as we step into the shoes of a new identity. The most striking change in wardrobe comes when you cease being a student and take your place in the work world, especially if it's in the traditional, corporate business world. Ideally, you will have begun to think ahead to this step in your senior year in college or have had some help from family.

Just as showers are given to brides to help with the needs of a new home, or to expectant mothers with baby needs, there really should be a shower for the soon-to-be grad. Graduation gifts are often monetary, which helps, but careful planning also helps—especially if you need to tackle a new wardrobe and a new apartment at the same time.

You're going to be shocked to hear this, and there is a whole chapter on accessories and shoes in this book, but here goes...for the record and for getting priorities straight. Even though the suit is the cornerstone of the wardrobe you are building, you don't pick the suit until you've got the right shoes!

All wardrobes are based on color groups; smart wardrobes are also built around comfortable shoes.

Yep, before you begin to select the individual elements of *any* new wardrobe, please step back and realize that colors, styles, and silhouettes need to be chosen *before* you go on your first shopping expedition. Life in the fashion lane does not begin with a purchase; it begins with some premeditated decisions.

Before you buy anything:

1. Pick the color group first. Stick to a basic such as black or navy, gray or brown, or even cranberry or red. Black is the easiest; navy is the trickiest because most navy blues differ subtly, making it harder to mix and match the pieces and expand your clothing vocabulary. Navy is also traditionally worn in the spring, although it will work all year round. In the last few seasons brown and gray have been fashion neutrals said to be more chic than black.

   You have many options in picking the color: black is always the safest choice, but regional tastes and climate may point you toward another shade. The point of the color is that it be a neutral and a foundation to a way of life.

2. Pick the shoes. The next thing after choosing the color is to choose two pairs of shoes in the same color group or a coordi-

Although there are some people who would say that the sole purpose of clothes is to please yourself, I disagree. Pleasing yourself is second; being appropriate to the situation is always first.

Expect the needs of your wardrobe to grow and change each year just as your life does, but never go broke over any one garment or any one look; don't be caught with a closet filled with clothes but nothing to wear because you are invited out to the opera.

Some people get it into their minds that they must own a certain item of clothing they simply cannot afford—say an Armani suit. They charge the suit and are saddled with debt for ages. Furthermore, the rest of the wardrobe now suffers because it doesn't measure up to the one good suit. The Armani suit becomes a stand-alone that causes more trouble than it is worth. Put your money into classics and spend less on accessories and trendy items.

nating color group. (If you've gone for the cranberry or red choice, do not pick black or brown or navy shoes. By selecting this palette you've struck out a little on your own and must follow through—you'll need red, cranberry, dark purple, wine, or some odd shade shoe that shows you are the master of these colors, not vice versa.)

You want to choose two different styles of shoes. The first should be a pump with a heel at 1½ inches or more that you can work in all day, not a pump that sends out a sexual message or a frivolous message. The second pair of shoes can be 1½ inches or less and should be sportier to go with trousers and more of a dressed-down look.

Shoes are vitally important because they are one of the few parts of your wardrobe that affect your health. You can't do your job if your feet hurt, nor do you want to damage young feet so that years from now you have a problem. It may sound silly to you now, but trust me on this: shoes are the foundation of life (see Chapter 7).

3.   Now you're ready for the suit. Bring the heels with you to try on with the suit choices. Ideally, your first purchase is a three-piece suit—jacket, skirt, and trousers in a classic style that you can expect to wear for years to come. The fabric need not be solid-colored; a small plaid or stripe or some textured weave is quite fine—but a print will not do.

With these three pieces, team up the tops. You will eventually want three blouses and one sweater to go with this suit:

- a classic business blouse in cream
- a matching or coordinating blouse, which can have a small print
- a shell, tank, or camisole that can cross over into evening and is also good for hot weather or high-anxiety days
- a sweater (probably turtleneck) that matches or coordinates with the suit and takes you into colder climates

When buying the suit, buy the best quality that you can afford. This does not mean a designer name. In fact, I'd ignore designer names and go for private label clothes—you want classically styled, well-made goods in high-quality fabrics. You don't really need a big name.

Shop sales, use coupons, go to outlets—do whatever it takes to maximize your dollars by investing in a well-chosen core group. Do a lot of window-shopping, do a lot of trying on, do a lot of learning—especially if this is a season with a change in styles. You do not want to buy the latest, hottest style; you are making an investment, not a fashion statement. Unless you are in the fashion business, trend is your worst enemy; see Chapter 8 for all about trends.

Please note: these ideas are not *just* for someone making the

Love vs. Need

I want to tell you about the chocolate chiffon Karl Lagerfeld dress marked down to $125 that I didn't buy but have never forgotten. I didn't buy it because I didn't need it. To this day that gorgeous gossamer dress has haunted me, but I hang on to the scientific processes that led me to walk away from the most beautiful dress at the most beautiful price of a lifetime in order to remind you about the bricks that build a lasting wardrobe.

I could not foresee the possibility of *ever* needing that dress and, believe me, I am a person who tries to be prepared for any possibility. Although I regret the choice, I have a small piece of self-righteousness that feels good about what I did. Not only didn't I need that dress, but in the four years that have passed since then, I've *never yet needed it* or had a real opportunity when I could have worn it. Regret is part of emotional shopping, not scientific shopping.

Had I bought that dress, I would have been increasing my dress-up wardrobe, not my workaday wardrobe. That would have been a boo-boo. I may have enjoyed wearing the dress and have gotten more than $125 worth of a thrill from it, but buying it would have been bad judgment. Only spend money to balance your wardrobe.

transition from student to Working Girl (or beyond)—every time you expand your wardrobe to include a new color, you should go through the exact same process. If the wardrobe is for a specific regional location, build it as appropriate for that part of the world, but still build around shoes and color blocks, then fill in with handbag and accessories.

When you are ready to expand, take a careful look at your budget. If you cannot afford to buy a second suit at this point, buy a skirt that goes with the jacket and will be appropriate for business appearances. You may also want to buy a flirty skirt that goes with the jacket that is right for dates. Depending on the cut of the jacket, you may want to consider a slim dress that fits under it— this should be a sleeveless dress and appropriate for both interviews and dinner dates. The right slip sheath can work, but be careful about how it fits and what message you are sending out.

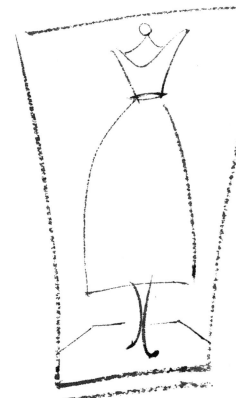

If you opt for a second suit, be certain it will go with the shoes you have chosen. If it's a second black suit, or same color suit, make sure it looks different enough from the first one that no one can mistake it for the *same* suit or think that all your clothes look alike. It's possible that you may want this suit to be a little dressier—it will be the call-back interview suit and can double as a date suit or a weddings and funerals suit. If the first suit had a straight and classic cut (as it should), the second suit can be a little more chic, more trendy, maybe even more curvy, while still being in total corporate good taste, of course.

If you've chosen black for your first suit, you may want to consider gray for the second suit. This will go with the black accessories you have, and the two parts can mix and match for more wardrobe expansion.

Only after you've bought the suits and other core pieces can you begin to think about the handbag and accessories to finish off your start-up wardrobe. When you have assembled the bulk of the wardrobe, you know what you look like and how you feel in the clothes; the final accessories are chosen to reinforce the statement and polish the look. The handbag especially must be chosen with care because it is so visible and it says so much about you.

An Aside About Red

Red is very popular in many regions and with many professional women; it is also a good color for a public appearance. But red is a "look at me" color, and you better have a very good reason to wear it, especially when you are starting out. If you do go for a red suit, it's usually better to use it as a stand-alone, not as a wardrobe cornerstone.

Budgeting a Wardrobe

Too many people make shopping mistakes by not being realistic about what they can afford and not being honest about what they need. After all, *need* is relative and is often emotional.

The less money you have, the more you need to spend it on good clothes and the more creative and flexible you need to be. If you haven't got access to alternative retail sources (see chapter 4), then keep your wardrobe small until you can afford to add more good pieces. Narrow in on a look that works for you (or a series of looks) and buy the best you can. Toss around money on silly things only after you've got the basics.

In a nutshell: buy less; buy better.

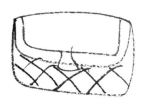

Therefore, there is a correlation between budget and breathing wardrobes, and there are ways to avoid big-time boo-boos:

- Never go into debt for the sake of a special occasion outfit.
- In fact, avoid buying a new ensemble for any one event (except maybe your high school reunion!) unless you can rationally absorb and use the pieces in real life.
- Never buy on layaway an item of cutting-edge chic that will be out of style before you pay for it.
- Never do more than one "bad thing" per month.
- Never throw money at a clothing mistake to make it better until you've lived with the problem, exhausted your creativity, and clearly found a sensible solution. It's often less expensive to give away the offending item than to try to make it better.
- Never buy a crazy color because you love it—buy and build wardrobes in color blocks that are coordinated to shoes, handbags, and accessories. Weird Jacket Science (page 108) applies only to advanced wardrobe enhancers.
- Never buy clothes to please a man (or any person other than yourself): buy only to please yourself and to project the image of yourself that you are most comfortable with.

Never build a wardrobe around an accessory unless you are very rich, a supermodel, or in the fashion business.

Defining the dollars-and-cents portion of your clothing budget very much depends on what stage in wardrobe building you are in currently, how much disposable income you have, what your personal style is, what your real (and imagined) needs are. However, you should never spend more than one-quarter of your monthly take-home pay on soft goods (clothing, shoes, etc.).

One of the best ways to stay on a budget—and to create a living wardrobe—is to work with a personal shopper or a regular salesperson or a small boutique where they know you and what you own.

A saleswoman at one of New York's big department stores told me that the client who spends $1,000 a month with her is her perfect client. I realized that I may spend $1,000 a month but I do it all over the place (all over the world, actually) and with no plan. If you work with one salesperson, or a store's personal shopper, your financial efforts are concentrated on the whole, you have an extra mind working for you, and you have someone who is helping you mind the budget. After all, if you go over budget, she will lose a client.

If you are looking to create a wardrobe from scratch, the most important thing is to shop around without buying anything (take a deep breath)—just use a notebook to jot down prices of the things you like and need to build your wardrobe. Once you see the difference between $39 shoes and $250 shoes you can better decide where to put your money.

The idea here is to avoid splurges and emotional purchases, which are the kinds of things that bankrupt you and derail even the best wardrobe-building strategy. Smart shoppers have a firm sense of value and cost vs. availability that tells them whether they need to shop at the beginning of a season and pay full retail, whether they should wait for sales (which are usually at the end of the season), or whether they can afford to hold out for hit-or-miss shopping at alternative and less expensive sources.

The most sensible budget allows for all three types of shopping and the progressive building of a wardrobe. But this system only works for people who like to shop…or have the time.

*It only takes money to buy expensive things; to **look** expensively dressed without spending much money is a far greater challenge.*

Ten Wardrobe Must-Haves

No matter how your wardrobe grows, changes, expands, or retracts, these are the icons that will get you through love, life, and work—even dress-down Friday. They are not in any particular order, so don't fret, and they are all clothing items. I've listed accessories in another list; there is also a full chapter on clothes and on accessories, so this is just to get the wheels turning. Note that because these items are icons, you should own the best quality you can afford and should trade them up only for better quality, rarely for fashion concerns. I've also provided parenthetically where I bought my example in this category, how long I've worn it, and what I paid for it. Hopefully this will help you see how icons amortize themselves.

1. **Navy blazer.** Lightweight wool classic, your choice in terms of style. Mine happens not to be a strict blazer cut but is a military-style jacket with brass buttons and epaulets. (I just bought mine this past year, Ralph Lauren/Polo purple label, at an off-pricer for $399.)

2. **Black cashmere sweater.** I prefer crew neck here because I think you can dress it up with a collar of pearls and it's more versatile. Later, add on more cashmere in neutral colors: turtleneck here is optional; I suggest cream or beige, but an interesting neutral such as blue-gray can work too. (Mine was inherited, but you can buy a two-ply cashmere sweater at any department store on sale for about $100.)

3. One pair of **black wool crepe trousers.** Must fit well, have pockets, and be classically styled to fit and flatter. Make sure the black matches your other blacks for mixing and matching. (Mine came from a major off-pricer for $99.)

4. One pair of **khaki chinos** or great-fitting blue jeans, depending on your figure and your ability to look great. (I buy men's chinos at Filene's Basement for as little as $14.99; mine were inspired by a Karl Lagerfeld design.)

5. Fabulous **cream-color silk blouse.** Must be dressy enough to go from office to opera. (I found mine, a wrap job that is flattering

to my figure type, at a resale shop for $35.)

6. **Black suit.** Just like Aunt Lynn and Barbara Walters said, you can't go wrong. The suit should be the type that can go from work to dinner, suitable for job interview and for first dates—in other words, not too sexy. Trouser suits are an option here; a three-piece suit is the best bet, though. (I had a classic-style blazer and trousers suit custom made in Hong Kong six years ago for $650.)

7. **Black jacket.** Not the suit jacket (above) and of a different texture, used to bridge day to night and to mix and match; must go with skirts and trousers. (I bastardized a black knit tricot suit, changed the buttons, and retired the skirt; I paid $224 for the suit at Loehmann's.)

8. **Black tube skirt.** OK, so this is a bit of a nod to fashion because tube skirts are in. But part of the point here is that the classic skirt is part of the suit and this skirt is more fashion for-ward. (As noted elsewhere, one came from a top designer—at top-dollar price—the other from a national retail chain.)

9. **Little Black Dress.** You may think this has been done to death, but you know you need one. Don't rule out a little black pants suit if that fits your lifestyle better. (I just got so bored with my basic Little Black Dress—it's eighteen years old, Sonia Rykiel, on sale for $150—that I bought an Armani black wool crepe dinner jacket with satin lapels, on sale for $699, to wear with trousers or tube skirt.)

10. **Black coat or raincoat,** depending on climate. (I've actually got three of these: I started with a $99 job from The Limited and have worked my way up over many years to a custom-made cashmere skimmer from Hong Kong.)

Weird Jacket Science

Navy blazers are classics because their lack of overtly trendy styling makes them neutral and timeless. But there's another way to go.

I have invested in a few very expensive, well-made, weird fashion jackets that are so unusual that they transcend time and trends, making them, in effect, classics. I wear them for years and always feel good because they're of good quality, distinctive, yet not "of the moment" (or worse, dated). This happens to work for my personal style; it may or may not work for you.

I should note that it is easy to make costly mistakes when experimenting with weird jackets and unusual colors. They often go with nothing when you thought they'd go with a zillion things; they're often too informal for a business situation where a simple suit is the solution—not an elaborate jacket, which may suggest you are begging for attention . . . or simply don't know appropriate dress.

Unusual jackets are also dangerous because they are memorable. You may not realize that other people see you and note what you are wearing, thinking, "Oh yeah, she's wearing that tangerine jacket again." Such memory would not accompany a navy or charcoal gray jacket. If you need to wear your jacket often, stick to something less notable.

However, if you've filled out your core wardrobe and can afford some nonwork-horse pieces, consider experimenting with Weird Jacket Science. Weird jackets are especially rewarding when they don't cost much money—one of my best cost £1 at a British flea market. At a price like that, who cares if

I can't wear it often? I've just scored a French blue polyester beaut with big plastic buttons and a white mink shawl collar at a funky vintage clothing shop, on sale for $38. This weird jacket will pay for itself in my lifestyle before I discard it and it makes the rounds again.

I was recently in the bar at the Hotel Ritz in Paris, to report on what the women were wearing, of course. I was turned out in one of my best suits, complete with a collar of pearls and big Chanel earrings and a verrrry expensive handbag. I thought my attire was perfect. I was wrong!

The dress of the day was weird jackets with nothing trousers, not much jewelry, and very expensive handbags, also in weird colors. You read it here first.

Five Accessory Must-Haves

1. Great pair of **loafers.** I'm going to leave the color up to you, but the point is that you can walk all day in them; they are probably a designer brand; they look good, and they reflect well on the wearer. Should go with trousers and skirts. (I use my Weird Shoe Color Theory, a variation on Weird Jacket Science, with my loafers: mine are magenta suede, bought on sale for $169 at Ferragamo's blow-out sale.)

2. **Fabulous handbag.** Not too small, not too big, can be expensive or simply look expensive. In summer you have more options with textures and materials. If you're just starting out, I'd go with the theory of a cheapie fun bag for summer and a killer black bag for all other seasons. Don't rule out the Weird Shoe Color Theory for handbags too. (Mine is Gucci, bought in Italy five years ago.)

3. Fabulous **small handbag** for dinner out, but not an evening bag. Preferably not black (or gold) but something interesting that will go with many things. A vintage piece is useful here.

4.   Great **tote bag.** Especially important for working women but good for shopping, for real life, for anyone, so you don't end up with too big a handbag. You can be flexible here, with season, with color, with texture, with attitude . . . but a shopping bag will not cut it. If you're carrying something heavy—like a telephone, a laptop, etc.—go for leather or something that can take the stress of the weight.

5.   **Pearls.** They don't have to be real but are worth being good. Also, work with your neck and face shape and body proportion. I wear two pearl necklaces because I have a long neck.

Growing Your Wardrobe

The easiest way to keep a wardrobe moving is to buy one suit per year or per season, depending on your budget and degree of style consciousness. This one unit will move you into the vogue.

The new garment is trotted out on those occasions when you need to show the world you too have new clothes and can change with the times, then is absorbed seamlessly into one of your existing color groups.

Your wardrobe should be refined academically at least twice a year, spring and fall, and probably four times a year if there are seasons where you live. This does not mean you should dash out to the mall on July 27—the day that the fall clothes always arrive in the stores—and buy a bunch of fall clothes. Proper preparation includes many rituals; these should be celebrated before you even begin to window-shop.

1.   Study fashion magazines, especially French fashion magazines because they report more on couture and good clothes. You don't have to buy these clothes, just use them to get ideas of what to do with the clothes you already have and to begin to assimilate the silhouette, shape, and accessories you will need for the new season. Clip pages from magazines.

2. From the clippings, make a list of targets for the season and assign them one, two, or three $ marks, signifying cheap, middle-of-the-road, or expensive. If I decide I need a pale green patent leather tote-style handbag, I will give it one $ on the list. If I can't find it in that price range, it's a no-go . . . or I must make a trade-off with another item on the list.

3. Get into the attic or the closet and take stock of the stock. Look over old, stored clothes to see if there's anything that's suddenly "right" again, anything that connects with the looks you have seen in the fashion magazines. Note: when I switch over my closet from one season to the next, I organize the clothes in my closet by season and by color.

4. Try on all the clothes you own that are appropriate to the upcoming season and the color groups you expect to wear. Everyone's figure changes, and everyone sees fit differently according to what's in style. True fact: an item can fit you the same way from one year to the next but look right one year and wrong the next just because of what the current silhouette is.

5. Prioritize what you already own. Last year's favorite outfit may be demoted or may hold its position. There could be a dark horse in there.

6. Looking at what you already own that's made the grade for the upcoming season, and looking at the clippings and your wish list, decide on your primary color group(s) for the season and then decide what items you will need to round out the existing items.

Wardrobe Checklist

Go through your closet, and try on and rate your clothes. Preferably try on the clothes as complete outfits, with hosiery and proper shoes. Then grade each outfit on:

FIT	SILHOUETTE & STYLE	COMFORT	ZIP

Zip? you are asking yourself—you haven't heard anything so quaint since the *Howdy Doody Show.* Well, to me, each outfit registers an emotional charge from boring to exhilarating—that's its zip code! I can love it one year and leave it another simply because of some psychological boost I get from the outfit. Zippity-doo-da!

Comfort is important in an outfit and can be quantified as a ratio of how good it makes you look to how long you will be wearing the outfit—I'll wear something uncomfortable but divinely gorgeous for a short period of time but not for a full day or under harsh working (or walking) conditions. All things are relative, so clothes and outfits can be rated by your own theory of relativity.

After surveying what you've got, you'll have a better picture of what you need. (There's more about expanding your core wardrobe in the next chapter.) When you begin to list the things you will supplement your wardrobe with, remember:

- Never buy an item that does not fit into one of your color groups.
- Never buy an item you don't love even though it's in the right color.
- Never buy an item you love to death and can't live without even though it doesn't go with anything you own.
- Never buy one piece of a whole, unless you know for sure that it matches and/or coordinates with your color group. Yes, you can buy a white blouse that will go with your black group. No, you shouldn't buy the navy blouse without the matching navy bottom because navies never match and it won't go with your navy wardrobe.
- Don't buy one perfect piece and then search for the rest of the outfit. Buy single pieces only when the item extends an *existing* collection (e.g., buying a sheath dress that matches the jacket and skirt you bought earlier in the season).
- Don't buy the wrong size because you plan to lose weight or you think you'll break in the shoes.

When you find a sale, **do:**

- Buy two of the same pair of shoes if they're on sale, they're proven winners, and you know you'll love the first pair to death eventually.
- "Stock up" on basics during sale times. Don't go nuts, but it's reasonable to buy six to twelve months' worth of things like panty hose and underwear as these are items you'll always need and they are less affected by fashion whims.
- Splurge on a very good quality classic, especially if it's on sale and if it expands your wardrobe—even if you don't specifically need the item. You will use it for years.
- Buy a cocktail dress, party dress, or even an evening gown if your lifestyle proves that you regularly wear such beasts and you find one you adore on sale that looks great on your figure. These are the kinds of things you never find when you need them or are forced to pay a lot of money for when you're under time pressure. If you are buying for the long haul, make sure you get a classic style that won't go out of fashion before you ever get to wear it. The Little Black Dress is always your best bet in this category.
- Make lists of items you have eyeballed at regular price that you want to come back for when the sales are on.

Shopping in Your Closet

I once interviewed Diane Von Furstenberg for an article for *Family Circle* magazine, and she taught me the concept of "Shopping in Your Closet." This was a true epiphany for me; it became such a big part of my shopping style that even my husband looks at me and says, Go shopping in your closet?

In my case, I go shopping in the attic. Many, many years ago, I interviewed Cheryl Tiegs for *People* magazine. She told me that she has a rule to keep control of her wardrobe—if she's faced with an item that she hasn't worn in one year, out it goes. I thought

"How fabulous! How smart!" and proceeded to weed through my closet like a madwoman. Out! Out! Out!

Within two years I was miserable and couldn't believe what I had given away. I vowed never to give anything away ever again. By the time I met Princess Diana, my attic was filled with plastic garment bags sagging with discards, with shopping bags heaped with shoes. These items weren't particularly organized nor were they ever explored they were just there as a reaction to my fiasco with the Cheryl Tiegs Rule of Simplicity.

Diana talked about saving everything too and how as trends came around she'd see pictures in magazines that would prompt memories of things she owned. She'd then go shopping in her closet to put together her own version of the look. She made the

point of how surprising it is each time you shop in your closet because you never really remember what you have, especially if you haven't seen it in twenty years, and you are often shocked and surprised (and pleased) that you already have something that is either perfect or will do just fine to complete a look.

Indeed, now that I know Diana's trick, I find that the most profitable shopping I do is when I browse through French fashion magazines to absorb the trends and styles of the catwalk. Invariably the photos trigger ideas within me of how to use something I already own.

I have reorganized the items in my attic by color group and by season; I do not have everything I own on a computer program, which is a great thing to do if you have the patience to do it and keep it up to date. The computer can't tell you what to pair with what, but it can tell you how many different pairs of black shoes you have and what style each is. Then each time you have an idea for a look you can consult your master supply list before you go out and buy something new that is similar to something you already own.

One of the best things about shopping in your closet is that it's doubly rewarding: you'll be shocked at what you find that you can use, which gives you the pleasure of rediscovery, and you will indeed save money.

chapter 6

Best Basics

Knowing the Good from the So-So

it's my bet that most of us, lacking Superman's X-ray vision, don't even try to see through things, and are therefore in the dark as to how most items of clothing are made—and why some cost more than others. We've all come to rely on labels, particularly designer labels, to tell us what is good or not; most people would rather buy an inferior garment with a statusy or designer label on it than an unbranded garment that was of equal—or even lesser—price.

Buying for label alone, however, has become far from a sure thing in these days of merchandising and marketing and bridge lines and franchise deals. Many brands that made their name and reputation for quality on superior goods have now watered down their lines (and sacrificed quality) in order to hit specific price points—and make big-time revenues. Invariably the margin (the pure profit zone between the actual cost of goods and the wholesale price a maker charges retailers) is greater on those bridge and diffusion lines, even though they are less expensive. Yes, volume has something to do with it, but just as significant is the fact that some makers realize greater profits from *reducing specifications,* that is, cutting corners on materials and manufacturing.

The result is that you can find a designer name on just about anything and, worse, finding a designer name on any garment does not mean you're necessarily getting your money's worth in terms of quality and design or workmanship.

It's time to set aside your preconceptions about fancy labels, big names, and tiny polo players on horseback and ask your purchases to step inside the examining room. Only by carefully examining an item can we have any idea of what we're paying for. In many cases, you need to be an expert to know what you are getting...or to employ tricky scientific tests that are beyond the mere lay shopper.

Never mind. We have ways.

Bare-Bones Fashion

From the times of the caveman—and cave woman, of course—up to the Industrial Revolution in the mid-1800s (1846, to be exact), all clothing was handmade. There were variations in quality even then, but essentially clothes were cut and sewn by hand and reflected this fact in their price and tailoring. Because of this, clothes also projected status and economic station.

With the advent of the sewing machine and later technological advances in the nineteenth and twentieth centuries, clothes could be made faster and more cheaply than ever before. The advent of the assembly line introduced the notion of mass-produced rather than custom-made and custom-fitted clothes.

As the machines continued to spin and turn, technology helped businesses figure out the best way to get the most from the fabric, how to cut corners to make money, and where to hold back on the quality in order to make money. A button-sewing machine recently advertised in a trade publication for shirtmakers guarantees that the way the machine sews on buttons will make the consumer falsely assume that the buttons have been hand-stitched. Take that, Ralph Nader! Eventually these new technologies would bring us to where we are now: unable to tell the difference in how certain garments are made, unable to judge which is a better product that will last, and what is worth what.

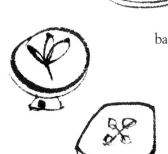

Furthermore, once there were ready-made clothes, they could be used to fool the eye of the beholder. Before mass production, clothing and social status/position were intertwined—clothes didn't make the man, they told the world all about the man who wore them: family background, social status, money, power, position.

Ready-to-wear meant the eventual arrival of a uniform that the great unwashed could adapt and adopt, fooling most of the people most of the time. These days, how well you choose your clothes is directly related to how well you can fool the people who assess what you are wearing. It might not be nice to fool Mother Nature, but you're invited to try to fool everyone else.

One fall, I had to appear at a magazine event with big-name editors and big-time advertisers and, frankly, I knew that my favorite suit of the moment, an inexpensive knockoff I'd bought in an off-price store, would not send the right message to this audience no matter how cleverly I had accessorized it. Because their discerning eyes evaluate garments—and personal style—every day, only the real thing would pass muster. In order to show I understood the lingua franca of their world, I felt I needed to fall back on the subtle status that only top designer labels communicate. (Hmmm, are my all-too-human insecurities showing?)

Willing to spend up to $1,000 for the security of this irreproachably appropriate garment, I actually walked into Giorgio Armani for the ultimate investment, but when I found that Armani suits started at $2,000 (and up), I decided to take another look at my classic Hong Kong suits, which turned out to be just fine. I vowed to return when the "good" clothes went on sale.

Skeletons in Your Closet

When you buy a garment, an accessory, or just about anything, you are paying for a certain set of variables:

- fabric
- construction
- site of manufacture
- designer name and marketing expenses
- store's overhead and marketing expenses

In terms of direct value to you, that will show on your back. Where your money counts *most* is in fabrication and construction; where your money counts *least* is in marketing expenses. However, because of the money spent on marketing, you are most likely to trust the firms that have built up public names and reputations—even though their garments and products may be no better made than those created by no-name firms. Learning to judge quality without a label is the key to knowing what you are really getting.

The Museum Quality Test

I personally happen to be the kind of person who overdosed on museums, churches, and operas by the time I was twenty. My idea of a good museum is one that doesn't make you pay museum admission in order to gain access to the gift shop.

Yet the truth is that you cannot begin to judge the quality of the items you buy until you have seen the avatar of quality, the genuine, top-of-the-line article. This means there are two laboratories you must work in: bona fide museums—which rarely let you touch the goods or look at the internal workings of a garment—and even more to the point, luxury stores, where any shop-

People laugh when I say this, but here goes: the best shopping spree begins in a museum.

per who looks serious about the goods will indeed be allowed to see, smell, feel, and even try on the best that money can buy. Yes, in my book (and this is MY book), luxury stores count as museums.

But first, start with the real deal. The world is filled with specialty museums that feature clothes, arts, crafts, decorative works, and jewelry exhibits. Look at the items that interest you; study books and catalogs to see how the items are made and finished.

Then go to luxury stores for a follow-up course in touching, feeling, and smelling—things museums often frown upon. The sales help in any luxury store worth its reputation will be delighted to give you a crash course in why their product is so superior and in how it is made. Take the time to learn before you make a substantial purchase.

The single best trick for assessing quality is to put a good example of an item directly next to a cheaper version. A cheapie $1,500 mink coat might look pretty good when you try it on in the store...but lay it next to a $10,000 mink coat and you'll quickly see the difference.

Of course, this is one of those exercises in life that is often easier said than done. But wait. You can often borrow an expensive item on approval or buy it on your credit card with the understanding that it can be returned for full credit to the account (not store credit!) if returned within twenty-four hours. Or switch the tables and buy the less expensive version, then go browse stores with the affordable item in hand, and compare the two, up close and personal. This way you can decide if you should return the less expensive copy or applaud your consumer savvy.

I'm not asking you to walk into Van Cleef & Arpels and buy a diamond necklace in order to compare it to a fancy faux. I do suggest that you use both sides of this coin (museums and luxury stores) to study the best and the brightest so

The Tiffany Touch

- Never buy an item of lesser quality without having seen and examined the best-made version in person.
- Never buy a packaged item without fully examining a sample to get some sense of what it feels and looks like, of how it's made.
- Don't forget to smell it—you can often smell the difference between good, bad, or indifferent. Chemical odors generally represent synthetic fibers or finishing treatments that mimic more expensive processes. Be sure you're not paying "vrai" prices for "faux" anything.

that you can know what excellence is and where you can and cannot cut corners. When you get really good at this game, you'll note that there are plenty of big-name firms with stellar reputations who cut corners all the time and don't give you a price break because they don't expect you to catch them at this very sophisticated game.

So get movin' and start learning things. Remember that marvelous slogan that Sy Syms, the New York bargain king, spouts off: "An educated consumer is our best customer"? He's right. Once you see (and learn) the difference, you may realize that the hard-earned $1,500 you are about to plunk down is best spent on a real good wool coat with fur trim or saved toward a $10,000 coat bought wholesale for $6,500.

Was it Ben Franklin who told us not to throw good money after bad? Sometimes the truth hurts, but though life may be short, remember that the time to enjoy a quality product is long. Which conversely means: a junky product won't last long and may not give you that extra psychological boost you get from owning and wearing something really special.

The Shopper's Dilemma

OK, so we know that a couture suit for $25,000 is a superior garment to the $500 suit sold in our local department store. But frankly, my dear, we can't give a damn because none of us can afford a $25,000 suit. In fact, while we might be able to buy a $500 suit, we'd rather get it on sale, at a discount store or off-price and pay, uh, $200.

The problem is, given a row of suits, or sweaters, or handbags priced from $500 to $150, or from $500 to $50 in the case of the handbag, how do we know which one is the deal?

Is a name a name or merely a trick?

Is the original price any indication of a sincere "original price" or has the suit been marked up to be marked down?

Is the item in perfect condition?

All advanced shoppers know that there are tricks to all levels of retail, and we can especially get confused when it comes to off-price shopping. Yet off-price shopping is just a window on all shopping and an allegory for the fact that we know all sorts of things are going on at all levels of retail. What we don't know is how to tell if we've found a find... especially when we don't recognize the name on the label. Step into my closet.

Suits

Aside from the Dress for Success Suit of the 1970s, which features a man-tailored blazer matched with a skirt, the construction of a woman's suit is different from a man's suit, because today's suit is usually a fashion item.

Indeed, while women's suits were the beginning of women's liberation in clothing—Egads, do you know what came next? Shirtwaists!—women's suits now come in a variety of formats, from the traditional feminized version of a man's suit (with a skirt, of course) to the soft pants suit, to the mix-and-match suit look assembled from separates. In between there are knitted suits, power suits (think *Dynasty*), dinner suits, and even formal suits, which may or may not owe their inspiration to a tuxedo.

A tailored blazer or classical trouser suit should indeed be made along the same guidelines as a man's suit. Yet few women invest in a suit, with either funds or emotions, the way a man invests in his suits. A man buys a good suit so that he can wear it to death for twenty years and never question how he looks. Most women can't stand the idea of wearing the same thing for twenty years, although a few sensible ones are now shaking their heads and most of us admit that we do have items in the closet that have given us twenty years, or more. I wear a black cashmere sweater that was my mother's, which I guestimate to be fifty years old, and I never tire of wearing it, but this is the exception, not the rule.

For the most part, men are not influenced by fashion nearly as strongly as women are. Women's suits are positioned with a more affordable price so that the shopper feels she has gotten her money's worth after a year or two.

If the main goal of the manufacturer is to express a trend and to sell a product at a palatable price, formal construction is the first thing to be modified. Consequently, fashionable suits are usually less constructed in order to allow for a softer build and a softer look.

Women's suits are more likely to reflect fashion trends of the moment and more likely to be chosen in a store for the fashion statements they make.

The length of the jacket, the color of the suit, the buttons, the cut of the jacket, even the length of the jacket sleeves—all are details in fashion configuration. Skirt styles are the leading factor in changing a suit silhouette.

Whether you are buying bespoke (custom-made) or off the peg, here are considerations to bear in mind when buying a suit:

- Each fabric type requires special treatment to make it perform best in your suit. Why did Chanel suits have little chains inside them? To weight down the knit jersey fabric and prevent it from rolling. What you are paying for is the maker's knowledge of the fabric he is cutting.
- Respect for those very fabrics is related to the lining and inner construction of the suit, both jacket and trousers or skirt. Lined trousers reflect a better-quality garment.
- An unlined jacket will not wear as well as a lined jacket, nor will an unlined jacket hide as many figure flaws.
- Knit jackets are rarely lined but often have some construction tricks built into them to keep them from rolling or stretching—look for the use of grosgrain ribbon or extra stitching, even small chains (Chanel).
- Women are much harder to fit than men because they have more curved parts and because the prevailing culture wants to see those curves—tastefully, of course. The variety of suit styles reflect this need: certain styles will be better for certain figure types.

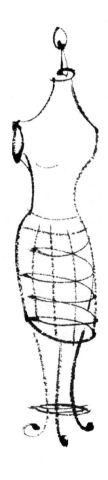

Women's suits are much more complicated than men's all right, but the basics of fit and construction are the same for both (so your honey can borrow these guidelines next time *he* makes a major suit buy):

- The shoulders are the most important indication of mood and fit.
- The jacket must fit smoothly across the shoulder blades and fall along the back without rippling.
- The jacket should button without making you look like Miss Nevada or Miss Piggy.
- Sleeves should hit the wrist knuckle unless meant to be worn at three-quarter length or rolled.
- The jacket should fit smoothly over the garment worn under it, be that a blouse, camisole, shell, or sweater.

- A half to a quarter inch of blouse or sweater should show at the cuff.
- The bottom piece of the suit, be it a skirt or trousers, should continue the line of the jacket without a break to the eye.
- Hosiery and shoes should also continue the line of the suit and the color tone in preferably the same hue; a dark suit should give way to dark leg and shoe; a light suit to lighter leg and shoe.

Note that many firms sell suit components separately so that you can buy a skirt in one size and the jacket in another to achieve a better fit.

The amount of money a person chooses to invest in a suit depends on the long-range plan for that suit—should it wear for years and look smart, or is it a toss-away fashion statement? Your wardrobe will ideally include some of both, and knowing which kind you're buying as you make your purchase will help you make the *right* choice at the right price.

While a high-quality, classically styled suit that will be a reliable performer for years to come is always a shrewd purchase, some suits accomplish more short-term goals, and as such make an equally valuable contribution to your wardrobe. Every season I try to make sure that my wardrobe contains at least one Gotcha Suit (see page 128).

A Gotcha Suit is intended to convey a combination of power and high style and affluence and good taste and elegance and sophistication, so that when I walk into that special meeting everyone can tell from a one-second glance at my suit that they can't mess with me.

The importance of such a suit is that everyone in the room understands the message; this means that the suit must be chosen to relate to the world of those at the meeting rather than simply

The Gotcha Suit

A few times a year I have to go to a meeting or a luncheon or some event when I want to look fabulous. I want to look rich and successful and power-ful, and I want each person who gazes at me to tremble in awe of what my clothes say about me. This is a business tremble, not a sexual tremble. Obviously, only a business suit will do. Yet it must be the right business suit, and I choose it independently from all my other clothes. This is my Gotcha Suit.

The Gotcha Suit can be a classic or a little more fashion forward; it can sometimes feature trousers. It's most often more successful if it's a designer suit, although you need not go into debt buying an outrageous suit just for one-upmanship.

I try to buy one Gotcha Suit a year, alternating the seasons—this means I expect to get two years of Gotcha Power from the fall suit and two years from the spring suit. After a period of years, a Gotcha Suit may be moved into the regular portion of my wardrobe and a new Gotcha Suit will be acquired. A girl can never have too many Gotchas.

to me on a personal level. While a man's suit makes a statement of stability and solidarity, a woman's suit is a costume created to evoke an emotional response in those who observe her. Of course, this ensemble cannot be so much a costume that the wearer doesn't feel comfortable or in control.

Comparing Goods

I have two suits that I am crazy about; each represents my state-ment suit from one of the previous fall seasons.

My "cheapie suit" is made by Finity; I got it at Loehmann's when the silhouette changed from baggy to slim and I needed to make a

The Interview Suit

The rules of dressing for a job interview at any point in your career are simple:

- Never dress better than your boss-to-be.
- Never dress counter to the company culture. Research the company culture.
- Don't wear costumes or native dress or symbols of ethnic pride unless you are auditioning for a costume-driven role that requires you to make that particular statement.
- Don't pick a busy print or stripes or loud plaids; solid is solid.
- Don't come on with a too-aggressive power look; speak softly and wear a silent suit.
- Don't wear too much jewelry, too many accessories, or anything that makes noise when you move.
- Don't wear stiletto heels or any shoes in which you wobble or sway.
- In short, simple is better. Less is more.

statement that said I was onto the shape of the moment. I got lucky; I bought a jacket, skirt, and matching trousers for about $225.

Note that I purchased three different sizes in order to get a good fit, including a size 16 jacket although I am normally a size 12 or 14. I was able to pull together all the pieces—hosiery, shoes, flower for the jacket, earrings...the whole nine yards. I lived in that suit for one season, and I thought I looked just fine, thank you.

My expensive suit is a trouser suit by Dei Trei, a small line once created by Louis dell Olio. (Dell Olio, as you may remember, used to design the Anne Klein line with Donna Karan.) I bought the suit on sale at a fancy department store for a total of $715, nearly

$500 less than the full retail price of $1,175. The suit was marked down by 40 percent.

I love this suit because not only is it gorgeous to look at—expensive fabric, unusual olive green/charcoal color—but it fits well and I feel like a princess in it. I can wear this suit to just about any event in the world and feel that comforting shield of power that comes from knowing I am beyond reproach.

The cheap suit looks OK on me because I carry it off with proper accessories and finishing touches. In fact, I'm being unfair to call it merely OK. It looks great. But at the end of the day it remains a cheap suit made good.

Less expensive lines are often sized small; in a cheapie jacket, you may need a large size.

The expensive suit looks like a million bucks, reflects on me in a positive manner, and is everything I always dreamed I could be in clothes. I love it, I love how I feel in it. BUT, this suit is made of such fragile fabric that I must baby it and will never be able to wear the suit to death.

As statements of personal style and power, both suits must be considered equally successful. But as investments, the cheap suit is still the clear winner; although it will go out of style long before the more expensive and more classic suit, it will more than pay for itself in the two to three years I will give it frequent use…and it will be worn to death. Later, its assorted parts will be absorbed into future looks and wardrobes.

Blazers and Jackets

A navy blue blazer is probably the single most important garment a man will own and can be equally important to a woman… depending on her own style. (See pages 105–107 for the ten best investment basics.)

No matter what the style of the blazer or jacket, in classic styles, you are paying for fabric first, then tailoring. In fashion garments, you are paying for cut, style, maybe even trim in equal measures. In the cases of very top designers—say Armani, Richard Tyler, Alexander McQueen, you are paying for cut first.

If the blazer is something you are going to wear forever, such as a classic navy blazer, always buy the best quality you can afford or trade yourself up every few years as finances allow.

Your Navy Blazer

Finding something special about a navy blazer is difficult because you don't want your blazer to be *too* special—at least to the naked eye. If it's too special, it become a fashion item; you are looking for classic style.

After you've narrowed down whether you want single-breasted or double-breasted, you simply need to buy the very best blazer you can afford. If you're flush with bucks, you may want a summer version and a winter version, chosen by the weight and texture of the fabric.

For most people, a light wool gabardine blazer will work just about twelve months of the year. If you spend time in a tropical climate, you may also want a navy linen blazer as a secondary blazer.

I have a girlfriend who owns only one item from Chanel, a navy gab blazer. At first I thought she was dumb—if you can buy one thing from Chanel, why would you buy something as boring as a navy blazer? Yet her wisdom was revealed over a two-week trip—no matter where we went, she trotted out that navy blazer, she looked great, and she *felt* great.

- If you consider only one fancy French designer garment in your life, make it a navy blazer.
- If you will own only one all-purpose, all-season blazer, depending on the climate where you will wear it most often, it should be a wool gab or twill that is tightly woven to take lots of punishment.
- The blazer must be fully lined.

Alec's Navy Blazer

My friend Alec is surely on the list of my ten best-dressed friends. He lives in Paris and travels constantly, picking and choosing only the world's best for his closet. I happened to notice his navy blazer not while he was wearing it, but while it was on a chair back, which allowed me to see the lining. And what a lining it was: a huge colorful print something like a tattoo with a Moschino Cheap & Chic logo, took up most of the space of the back panel. You couldn't help but burst out laughing and then marvel.

Alec explained that he actually bought the jacket *because* of the lining, saying, "If you have to wear something as boring as a navy blazer all the time, at least you should have the inner satisfaction of a secret giggle, knowing within yourself that your jacket is not what it seems."

- If you expect to get only a few years out of the blazer, the interior construction is less important than if you want twenty years of steady wear—an unconstructed blazer can take about five years of steady wear.
- Give the buttons on the blazer your sternest evil eye; consider replacing them. Many a cheap blazer has come alive with the addition of decent buttons.
- Check the shanks on the buttons; reinforce buttons before they can fall off.
- Beware of the shoulders and the lapels, the two areas where fashion come into play and can date a jacket, even a classic like a navy blazer—neither should be too wide.
- Consider owning two navy blazers, one of excellent quality and one of lesser quality so that in situations of high risk for damage, you can wear the lesser-quality piece and not be hysterical if something happens to it.

With fashion jackets, the cut and design often make a style statement that is equally as important as the fabric and the fit—leaving much more room for degrees of quality. A cheapie fashion jacket will always look cheap, whereas an expensive jacket will go out of style before it wears out.

A fashion jacket can be created in any number of styles, some of them reflecting the vagaries of the look of the moment. The more classic the style, the greater the chances that you will wear it for a period of years.

There is a good bit of difference between a jacket and a suit jacket—in most cases, the suit jacket is only to be worn with the suit bottom and to take the stress of business wear. A stand-alone jacket must be tougher because it will be used often.

When suits are sold as a multipiece outfit rather than as separates, the maker is very much aware of the fact that the entire unit must carry a palatable price, especially in mass-merchandised lines. Break apart the suit concept and figure that a no-name basic skirt (or trousers) can be worn with a great jacket; you'll soon see why it makes sense to put more money into the jacket than the suit, and a world of choice and possibilities opens up. When choosing a jacket, therefore, it pays to ask yourself:

If you can't afford a high-quality blazer, consider a lesser-quality one, then change the buttons to higher-quality ones.

- how many things you own that will go with the jacket.
- whether you have to create entire outfits from pieces not yet found and how hard (and costly) it will be to find said pieces.
- if there is a direct correlation between the price, the quality, and the longevity of the jacket in terms of style or color.
- whether the jacket brings your current wardrobe into the vogue by highlighting a new trend that helps update pieces you already have.

- if the jacket is the kind of garment that can take the stress of multiple uses or is just for certain types of events or appearances.
- if the jacket transforms day clothes you already own into an evening look.
- whether the jacket gives off the message you want the world to absorb in the few seconds you will be assessed by total strangers.

Shirts and Blouses

Ascot Chang, one of the most famous gentlemen's shirtmakers in the world, boasts that it takes thirty-one different measurements to make a single shirt and that there are twenty-three stitches per inch in sewing the garment. My tailor, Peter Chan, says there are nine different measurements in his shirts and twelve checking points. There are twenty-six stitches per inch in one of Peter's shirts.

Indeed, the number of stitches per inch is one of the easiest handles to grasp for a quick judgment on the quality of a blouse or a shirt—fifteen to eighteen is an acceptable number on a machine-made, mass-produced shirt, anything under eleven is garbage.

Custom-Made Shirts: If you're used to seeing men's dress shirts piled up in discount stores with plenty of choice at a reasonable price, then you will be confounded by the choices a man makes when he has a bespoke shirt made. There are usually fifteen different types of collars to choose from, a variety of cuffs, and then books and books of fabric swatches.

A custom shirt will have twelve to twenty measuring and checking points for fit so that the shirt not only fits but moves with the body, stirred but not shaken. Shirttails are sufficiently long that the shirt will never come out of the trousers; there are shirtmakers who make shirts with a snap crotch (à la Donna Karan) to ensure that they don't fly away.

Mass-Produced Shirts: To judge the quality of a mass-produced shirt or blouse, take these factors into account:

- Quality of the fabric—100 percent natural anything is considered a superior product, although in some climates or some situations (traveling for business, for example) a cotton-polyester blend may be preferred. However, a blend is never considered top quality.
- Origin of the fabric can be factored into the quality equation. British or Italian cotton is considered superior to Chinese cotton and costs more. Fabric weave per thread count (how many threads per inch)—just as in sheets—is the telling factor in quality in cotton shirts; more expensive mass-produced shirts have 50 to 80 threads per inch, whereas Sea Island cotton, considered the finest, has 140.
- Stitching of the garment—stitches should be small and uniform. The more stitches per inch, the better the quality of the shirt.
- Fabric at the cuffs and along the yoke should be pleated and lying flat, not gathered or tapered—pleats allow for more movement in a smoother manner.
- Buttons should be mother of pearl.
- Buttons should be cross-stitched, or if on soft, spongy fabric like silk or satin, shanked.
- The collar should be stitched evenly and lie flat—if it puckers, pass it up.

Trousers

We're talking about cut and sewn trousers, which means they are made of flat woven fabric, not knits. The fit of trousers is primarily focused on the bum; if the trousers do not fall away from the rear end at the halfway point, they do not fit properly—or they are jeans. Or, to put it more simply: jeans hug the rear;

trousers do not. If trousers fit in the rear, everything else can be altered to fit.

Once you've checked the bum, the next important factor is how the waist is built and reinforced. It should be reinforced with inner linings and a no-slip ribbon or band that keeps the waistband from stretching and losing its shape while grabbing hold of the shirt to keep it tucked in. If no interfacing used in the waistband, a stay as simple as a grosgrain ribbon will help keep the waist true to size.

Pleats are one of those things that go in and out of style on women's trousers; if they are present, pleats should lie flat and not pucker or gather. Trousers do have a center crease on each leg; note that jeans do not.

Jeans

If you think this is a simple subject—think twice. There are label wars going on out there over the enormous amount of money spent annually on good old blue jeans. These days, a pair of jeans can easily cost over $100, and jeans are cut in various ways to convince people—especially women—that there's a significant difference between all those brands and all those bucks.

Jeans were first made of canvas, not denim, by a twenty-two-year-old guy named, you guessed it, Levi Strauss. These trousers were created for miners during the 1849 California Gold Rush, and were made from the same fabric used for covered wagons. Compared with standard trousers of the times, these moved, they were sturdy, they were, uh, blue collar, and they weren't actually trousers—an amazing breakthrough.

Soon Mr. Levi Strauss modified his pants from canvas to denim, a French cotton serge from the town of Nîmes in Provence. Because of its provenance, the fabric was thus named "de Nîmes," which was eventually shortened to the term we know today. (More fun etymologies: a similar fabric was also made in India, home to a large cotton textile industry; the fabric was called *dungi* there, hence the term *dungarees*. Indian sailors wore the *dungi*, but soon other sailors wore them too, including Italian sailors from Genoa. Hence the terms *jeans,* a bastardized form of *that* town's name.)

While a jeans cut is now available in myriad fabrics with assorted style details, basically, jeans are about only one thing—the wearer's behind. A good pair of jeans is judged on its ability to lift, shape, and mold the derriere of the wearer. Bottom line. End of story.

Designer jeans fall into a unique category—they cross brilliant marketing with the promise of fabulous fit. Sometimes designer jeans are also innovative—Ralph Lauren and Calvin Klein each have dozens of different styles and cuts, and the husband-and-wife team Marithe and François Girbaud in France have always done groundbreaking work in blue jean fit and fashion. DKNY, Versace, and Liz Claiborne make jeans.

There is a lot of similarity between a brassiere and a pair of jeans.

Aside from these designers who have associated their names with jeans, there are also jeans makers who produce such a specialized product that their jeans are considered fashion items.

About twenty years ago I wrote a story for *People* magazine about what was "in" with teens in Beverly Hills, and I discovered Guess? jeans, which were cutting-edge at the time. Since then, Guess? has become a major design and retail lifestyle force in this country, with many new entries, such as Diesel and Lucky's. I actually remember that one maker of jeans used a specialty gimmick to sell his jeans—a small diamond inset into the rear pocket!

Certain brands in jeans carry on with the type of marker they use in their ready-to-wear, so that Liz Claiborne is known for a

Designer Who?

The term *designer jeans* is actually inappropriate. Whereas the designer may indeed bring some ideas to the basic concept and have more to offer than his fancy label sewn onto the jeans, the true beauty of a pair of jeans is in the match between the construction and your body. The success of Calvin Klein jeans convinced many consumers that a talented designer holds some divine secrets of cut or pattern for which the public can be convinced to pay extra bucks. Esoteric jeans makers in New York and parts of Europe earn upwards of $80 per pair because their designer jeans are rumored to hug the butt or the hips in just the right way. A design team in New York's East Village sells jeans at over $100 per pair and has a waiting list. And it is true that you may find a designer line that fits you like a glove. But remember, after fit, jeans—and designers—sell attitude. Don't laugh. You know that Calvin's attitude is a little bit naughty, but every other brand has an attitude too. The attitude comes across in the ad campaign and on the floor to help sell the customer.

"missy fit" whereas DKNY jeans have a "contemporary fit." If that's Greek to you, a missy fit tends to be shorter and fuller.

The only real factors in the success of any jeans are:

- fit in the rear
- fit in the crotch
- fit in the thighs
- style of the cut in the legs

Fit in the rear and hips can be somewhat related to the form of closure, which is why snap-front jeans are still popular. And, of course, the unspoken reason that nothing came between Brooke and her Calvin's was that these particular jeans fit so snugly in the rear and the crotch that if she wore underwear you would see unsightly ridges and panty lines.

Nowadays, jeans also come in high-rise and low-rise versions and even male/female versions, since jeans were not originally made for women and did not adequately address the concepts of hips and/or waist.

"Women are built with hips; it's normal!" screams a woman in a televised jeans commercial that airs during the morning talk shows. The brand she represents is cut specifically to allow for hips and waists, something Mr. Levi Strauss didn't have to think about when designing for miners way back when. It's this kind of marketing that brings a shopper to try a specific brand.

In the pursuit of a perfect fit, some makers have added stretch to their fabric although the bulk of jeans out there are made of plain old cotton denim. Because it is cotton, denim does shrink, so washing jeans can be counterproductive for anyone with a "just so" pair of jeans—once you get 'em perfect, consider dry cleaning. But don't think that stretch is just for teenagers; stretch may give a middle-aged body just the boost it needs.

Because worn jeans have a certain shape and style built into them from previous wearings, there is a large market in used and

Metric Conversion Chart: Jeans Inseam

28" inseam = 71cm
30" inseam = 76cm
32½" inseam = 82½ cm
34" inseam = 86cm

vintage jeans. Some women will pay $80 to $100 for a pair of properly worn-in jeans.

The point in buying jeans is not what they cost or what kind of label is on your tush—it's fit, fit, fit. Don't pay high prices for fit that's not there; don't think you have to pay a high price to get a good fit.

Sweaters

I can think of only one person who has made a career out of a single sweater—no, make that two—Marilyn Monroe and Sonia Rykiel. Let's work with Sonia here because while she now has an entire range of women's ready-to-wear, men's ready-to-wear, kids' clothes, fragrances, and everything else that comes with the big time.

I own several Sonia sweaters, including one twin set. The twin set is over twenty years old; it is as chic and special and unusual and rich today as it was when I bought it on sale all those years ago. More recently, in a fit of divine madness, I plunked down about $500 for a blue tunic sweater at Sonia's boutique in Paris. Now, five years later, I've gotten constant pleasure from that tunic—it's always fresh, it's always chic, it always looks rich, I always love wearing it. That makes it a $500 bargain and a good investment.

Sweaters, especially mass-produced sweaters, aren't made very differently from each other, so the only thing you are paying for in an expensive (non-cashmere) sweater is the fashion statement. Few sweaters can be identified by designer, so forget the name on the label. Pay only for the design and its longevity.

The perfect sweater requires three ingredients: chilly weather, good-quality wool, and long winter nights in which to knit. But the world is filled with less-than-perfect sweaters because now we have knitting machines and man-made fibers. These are not bad things, and don't let anyone convince you that they are. You just need to learn what you're paying for.

Sweaters actually date back over two thousand years and have been found in Egyptian tombs; sweaters as we know them today grew out of medieval times when there was a knitter's guild that spun flax to gold, more or less. The Industrial Revolution modernized the business, and sweaters moved into two specifically different camps of production: the small cottage industry of high-quality, usually handmade, specialty sweaters and the mass-produced sweaters made to warm the shivering masses of humanity.

Never buy a sweater for the label.

Today's sweater prices are based on:

- the fiber used
- who made it
- how

Cashmere (pages 144–147) is a separate issue, since in that case the fiber itself determines much of the price and value of the sweater.

Most sweaters, even expensive cashmere sweaters, are machine-made and mass produced. The most expensive sweaters are handmade and made of natural (possibly rare) fibers. Man-made yarns came into vogue after World War II, and they are a boon for those who are allergic to wool; they also make machine care more of a possibility, although why anyone would machine wash a sweater is beyond me.

Most important, man-made fibers can deliver softness at a soft price. In fact, if you gave me a blindfolded test of two sweaters, I'm not at all sure I could tell a cashmere sweater from a fancy acrylic sweater by feeling them (see Sweater Rationale, page 146). To pass judgment on the value of a mass-produced sweater consider only:

- fiber
- construction
- novelty

Wool: As a natural fiber, wool has a lot going for it; it's warm, it's resilient, it is somewhat fire retardant (in that it's slow to burn…but it does and will burn), it breathes, it wicks, and it has some sense of memory—it can bounce back from being stretched and it can be blocked to a new size.

Baa, Baa, Black Sheep?
A Dictionary of Woolies

Alpaca: Alpaca comes from a llama, not a sheep, and is most often harvested in South America. It's light and fluffy and much warmer and stronger than wool, which is why it's often used in coats. Note that even a garment labeled 100 percent alpaca usually has some wool woven in to hold it together, as the fibers are long and silky. Legitimately the garment must contain 85 percent alpaca to be labeled 100 percent alpaca. Note that alpaca, like wool, feels itchy to many people.

Angora: Some people may confuse angora and alpaca because of the long silky fibers, but angora is actually rabbit hair. The fibers are much shorter, so they add to loft and hand but make sweaters far more fragile.

Boiled Wool: This process is most often used in England to produce a specific look and durability in wool—tight, tough, and uh, boiled.

Cashmere: It's a goat! And it's not a coincidence that half this word spells cash! See pages 144–146 for specifics.

Chenille: Not a wool at all, but a treatment that produces velvety texture on fibers of cotton, silk, or synthetics.

Lamb's Wool: Wool from the first shearing of a sheep is called lamb's wool; it's rarely used in sweaters.

Mohair: Back to goats! Long fiber, very strong, can be confused with angora (from a rabbit) partly because it comes from an angora goat and partly because of the texture. Often used in jackets and blankets because of its durability.

Shetland: Slightly brushed fibers give a specific hand to this wool.

Vicuna: We're back to llamas now. The vicuna hails from Peru, and its fur is sheared once a year so that the most prestigious mills in Italy can make it into coats. Vicuna is banned in the United States because it is endangered. It's also about five times more expensive than cashmere.

Wool Blends: Wool can be mixed with other fibers, sometimes cotton but often man-made, to make the wool less itchy, to make it more lightweight, and to make it even more durable.

Like all natural fibers, wool comes with its share of pedigrees based on the type of sheep the wool was gathered from and how and where the wool was combed and processed. The finest wool is traditionally merino, named for the breed of Australian sheep from which it is gathered—sweaters and clothes made of merino wool are usually marked "merino wool" and can be expected to cost more because of this pedigree. Also note that many fibers made into sweaters, coats, blankets, and shawls are not really wool and therefore don't come from sheep.

Real wools, which do come from real sheep, are graded and sorted according to the type of sheep they're from and even the part of the world in which those sheep are raised. Just like a fine wine, a fine wool is very much related to the land and the food source that was transformed into the end product. There are actually hundreds of different breeds of sheep, and even those that are shorn for woollies are divided into categories by the coarseness of their coats. The softer the wool, the higher its value in garments. Coarse wool is tightly coiled and is best for carpets.

Cashmere: Cashmere is a type of fiber, but also a state of mind and luxury. Cashmere clothes fall into a category of their own. If anything drives me crazy, it's shopping for a cashmere sweater and finding similar products that range in price from $99 to $499. Certainly these aren't equal cashmeres and surely there's more than profit, label, and store overhead in the different pricetags.

For the most part, the difference lies in these factors:

- the provenance of the cashmere itself
- the way the wool has been treated and sorted
- the way the cashmere is combed and milled
- the number of strands of cashmere, called plies, that are woven together
- the finishing details of the garment and how much has been hand-stitched

Let's go for plies first. A ply is a strand of cashmere wool, ready to be knitted into the garment. One-ply cashmere is the least expensive; two-ply cashmere is the standard weight for regular winter wear; four-ply cashmere is rather heavy, and eight-to-ten-ply is rare and used in jackets, heavy outerwear, or ski garments.

The plies are spun together to create a yarn filament; a two-ply strand is smoother and stronger than a one-ply strand. After that, however, the number of plies does not increase the tensile strength or quality of the garment, only the weight and bulk… and therefore the warmth and density.

Memo from the Lonely Goatherd

Yodel-lady-whooo: how many goats does it take to make a cashmere garment?

1 goat = 2 pairs of socks
1 goat = 1 scarf
2 goats = 1 average crewneck sweater/woman's size
3 goats = 1 average crewneck sweater/man's size
4 goats = 1 two-ply dress
15 goats = 1 cape
24 goats = 1 coat

Cashmere itself is graded in quality, not only by where it comes from geographically but by where it comes from geographically on a specific goat. While most cashmere is Chinese, after it leaves China it can end up in any number of factories around the world. It's what happens next that adds to the cost; Italian and Scottish cashmeres are the world's finest mostly because of what they do to the cashmere once they have it.

The best mills sort the cashmere fibers very carefully and reject a portion of them as too short and too weak. This inferior cashmere may be blended or sold to others who aren't so picky. The cashmere is then combed and carded and made into yarn. This is in turn made into sweater parts that are joined—by hand for good cashmere. Construction in cashmere is related to stretch and fit. Fit should remain stable, whereas stretch is a bad thing—you don't want a sweater that will stretch out of shape.

The word *cashmere* comes from Kashmir, where goats with very silky, warm fur are found in higher altitudes. Goats are not sheared like sheep; they actually shed their coats through molting. To harvest the crop, the goats must be hand-combed.

Alas, the hairs are of differing lengths and textures and must be sorted; furthermore, there are two grades of cashmere based solely on whether the goat is wild or ranched (domesticated). The longer, sharper hairs are called guard hairs. A top-notch cashmere coat will have less than 5 percent guard hairs in its construction; a fine cashmere sweater will have fewer than 1 percent guard hair. The fewer guard hairs, the higher the quality of the cashmere.

In the best grade of cashmere, there are some forty steps that go into production of a finished sweater. There are also some cultural preferences to the steps in readying cashmere for market. Italian cashmeres go to market as the softest available; Scottish cashmeres are not rinsed as often in the milling process and therefore get softer with wearing. Go figure.

When choosing a cashmere sweater, especially in a classic style, it pays to shop both the men's and women's departments. Even though a man's sweater usually takes more fiber than a woman's, men's sweaters often cost less than women's. A woman may particularly score during an end-of-season sale when a color that is too fashion forward for a man to wear is left behind at a bargain price.

Sweater Rationale

I must wear a lot of scarlet; otherwise I would not own so many similar sweaters: a dark claret Scottish cashmere man's sweater with a polo neck; a Calvin Klein hand-loomed tony little poor-boy sweater in rose; and a brick, oversized sweatshirt-style crewneck from Kikit, which two winters ago was that one item I seemed to have grafted to my skin. (This year it's something else, thank God.)

As I hope I've already made clear, I seem to need *all* of these extremely similar (yet alarmingly dissimilar) sweaters for the choices they offer me. One's sweater wardrobe is seldom limited to a plain old sweater but is a selection of sweaters based on necklines, body fit, fiber, and suitability for the event and context in which it will be worn. In many cases, the sweater is the message.

Sweaters also work in fashion cycles. Have you noticed the re-emergence of the twin set in the past few years? How about the velvet-trimmed sweater, as influenced by Voyage of London? The poor-boy sweater? And I haven't touched on chenille. My collection of chenille sweaters has grown from the first must-have-to-show-I'm-trendy piece to a total wardrobe for every day of the week…and then some. Yet I have no question that they will eventually pass into fashion limboland. Then, of course, I'll just have to buy more sweaters.

But don't dismiss classic sweaters. I have one specific sweater that I have lived in for decades. I've worn my best sweater—Mom's crewneck black cashmere from the 1940s—with trousers and a jacket, with a chiffon skirt to a black-tie event, as part of a suit, and with jeans. My attachment is not sentimental. This is a copy point: the right classic sweater can be most versatile and will certainly do the trick even for a black-tie event. You can argue classics versus chenille and lose every argument if you don't vote classical.

Handmade and Novelty Sweaters: There is a trick in the use of the words *handmade* and *handknitted*. A "handmade" sweater often means that the pieces of the sweater were made on a knitting machine but were joined by hand, whereas "handknit" means the knit-one, purl-one was done by a human being.

A knitting machine produces a much more even, uniform stitch. What you are paying the big bucks for is that uneven effect garnered only when one person sits down with two knitting needles and creates. The most difficult of these creations involve counted patterns, so that price is not solely based on the hand-knitting but also on the difficulty of the knitting style.

Most handmade sweaters are bulky, and part of their charm is their ruggedness; they are often most useful as outerwear or over-layers worn over camisoles, silk shells, or even turtlenecks.

Novelty sweater is actually a trade term applied to sweaters made special by a novelty feature, most often in the trim: sweaters with fur collars, sweaters with hearts knitted into them, sweaters with ribbon or studs—you get the drift here.

Buying Sweaters

- If you like oversized sweaters, consider shopping in the men's department.
- If you're petite, consider shopping in the kids' department.
- A sweater that already shows signs of wear while still on a hanger will never wear well in real life. If it's for continued use, give it a miss.
- Odd colors are the first to get marked down; basics are slow to be marked down.
- Sweaters cannot be successfully altered to great extent, although sweaters made of natural fibers can be blocked to shrink or stretch approximately one size.
- Sweaters fit differently based on style and make—even though they come with sizes, sizes are far less specific, and so is fit. Try on a sweater not only for fit but for fit the way you plan to wear it (over trousers, under a suit jacket, and so on).
- The best sweater styles are those that can be layered. Look for classics that mix and match with your wardrobe.
- Check out offbeat sources for novelty sweaters or classics; even cashmeres show up at flea markets and yard sales.
- Sweater bodies are as varied as the human body. Some are classics; others come and go with trends. Depending on your own figure type, certain styles will or won't work on you. It's OK to break the rules every now and then, but don't push it, especially with a revealing sweater.
- Cashmere is luxurious, but it also demands care and can be very hot. Colder climates may overheat offices and malls; you can really suffer in cashmere. Think twice before succumbing to the luxury.

Lingerie

When I was growing up, we called lingerie underwear. For most of my life, "lingerie" has been a foreign language and a foreign philosophy. I still remember the chagrin of my freshman year in college when I undressed to reveal my plain white cotton padded bra from the bargain bin at Solo Serve ($3.99) and little-girl white cotton panties (99 cents) while my roommate disrobed nonchalantly to reveal a pale turquoise *parure* (as the French would say, otherwise known as a matched set) of demi brassiere and bikini pants edged with taupe lace.

I discussed my envy with my mother, who dismissed the whole notion as pure fantasy, nonsense, and bad values. "Why tie up your money in something that no one can see?" she demanded.

There is an answer to this question. Lingerie helps you feel good about yourself; it helps you feel powerful and wonderful.

Underwear is not about sex. I used to think it was about being good to yourself, about self-image and self-esteem. Now I know better. The world's finest underwear is about power. That's why Mom dresses us in Big Bird or cartoon-printed knits—kids have no power. And that's why we turn to lace and thongs and little bits of silk and satin—for the sensual power they awaken within us, not for what they do to someone else who may or may not be paying attention.

Along the way, without going overboard, girls just want to have fun. In lingerie, the tangibles you are paying for include:

- fit and lift
- fabric content
- comfort
- novelty

It's been said that a large percentage of women (globally) wear the wrong size brassiere. I have no problem accepting this because I certainly don't try on every bra I buy and I will usually sell out both comfort and fit if I can get a good buy on a gorgeous piece of fluff that makes my heart sing.

There's a correlation in my mind between how I buy shoes and how I buy brassieres, which is interesting since they are the only two pieces of clothing with exacting technical specifications related to fit and function.

A serious brassiere should be purchased in the same way that a fine pair of shoes is sought and bought.

Step into the Parisian shop of Hermione Cadole, whose grandmother invented the brassiere for the girls of the Crazy Horse Bar, and she will quickly explain that Americans don't know anything about making brassieres, nor do American customers know anything about fit. The proper brassiere lifts and separates the bosom; the work is done in the cup not in the strap.

The cost of a brassiere depends on its construction, from an inexpensive one-size-fits-all elastic-and-cotton number to a custom-made, hand-sewn model. (Yes, there is such a thing as a bespoke bra—the Queen of England wears one.) You won't find an old-fashioned corset shop at the local mall, but they discreetly exist in America and in every major city in Europe, where aristocratic women have long gone for sublime fit and contour. Movie stars also use specialty corset shops; the wrong brassiere has been known to bring production on a television show to a stop.

So while most of a brassiere's price reflects the intricacy and quality of its construction, fabric (silk or fine lace) and novelty (extra lace, pearls, etc.) will also add expense, as will hand-stitching, or hand-tucked silk, handmade lace, etc.

Partly related to the construction are two other important factors—the size of your own bosom and the type of outward look you want. A variety of treatments are now socially acceptable: many undergarments can make it look like you aren't wearing a bra except for the lift, while others mold you into a new shape or contour you into seamless softness.

The best bra does what your body needs it to do and what your clothes demand that it do. The larger the bosom, the more difficult it is to get a good fit.

As for knickers, aside from designer labels, you pay mostly for fabric and for lace, but cut and drape do raise the cost as well. Silk and handmade lace bring up the cost enormously, although every discounter sells silk panties for around $10 a pair … or less. Many luxury undies are cut on the bias, which uses more fabric and raises price—a bias-cut garment will hug the figure better.

Modern manufacturers have convinced women, especially American women, that you buy underwear as a fashion statement having nothing to do with need. Still, the dollars and cents of it is in volume, so the best-selling colors are white, black, and nude. Everything else is fashion, depending on the "in" colors and fabrics and textures. Such styles are transient and will be dumped at discounters some months after they don't move from a retail floor or factory showroom.

While you can never count on what may turn up at an off-pricer (or whether you'll find what you need in your size), I've seen every major French brand and some of the most famous Italian brands (yes, even La Perla) show up at my neighborhood T.J.Maxx. The asking price at this off-price source is $29 per bra, a far cry from the $250 original price.

But if brand name or internationally cut lingerie is your preference, it can often be found at discounters in America. The trick here is to get an education, because most American shoppers don't know the powerhouse brands from Europe and therefore won't know a steal when they see one. Some names to look for include La Perla, Cadole, Aubade, and Rosy.

Read French fashion magazines at the hairdresser or the library

European Bra Chart

If you are shopping in Europe or buying European brands in the United States, you may have trouble figuring out your sizes, as a metric measurement is used. Cup size is the same as in the United States. (*Bonnet* is the word for cup in French; it is measured with the alphabet just as in the United States.) The back measurement, however, is in centimeters; here are translations:

US	FR
32	85
34	90
36	95
38	100
40	105

(or subscribe; call 800-363-1310 for a price list from a French Canadian firm that handles all the big French magazines) to see the ads for the large lingerie firms so you can recognize the names when they turn up at your favorite off-pricer.

chapter 7

Makers and Breakers— Accessories

R o m a n c i n g   t h e   D e t a i l s

whoever said clothes make the man was wrong. It's accessories that are the telling mark these days. *Shoes* make the man—or woman—not clothes.

How you are put together makes a big difference in how you are perceived by the ever-watching public, but you can often fake it with your clothes. Accessories, on the other hand, are dead giveaways to your station in life.

Naturally, I have two philosophies regarding the fine art of accessories, and while they may seem contradictory, they are actually just two sides of the same coin and can be used side by side as you build your wardrobe.

- I believe big accessory statements are so important that they are worth saving up for—for a small percentage of the items in your wardrobe, you should buy the very highest quality (and status) you can afford, *but* . . .
- I also think you can cheat in fashion/cutting-edge areas where it's bad business to tie up big bucks to prove you have the latest color, style, or trend. Buy cheap, disposable accessories of the moment to fill in a wardrobe and make trend statements.

You've just gotta know when to hold 'em and when to fold 'em.

Style and Statements

Because accessories are such a major part of how we change our looks and how we observe fashion rituals, styles, and trends, they tend to come into use in waves, sort of a sub-tide of fashion. I've seen chain-style handbags come into style twice (they're really murder on a fur coat); I've seen tying an Hermès scarf on the chain or strap of a handbag be an absolute must to being so passé that I do it just to be ornery. Backpacks have come and gone twice (quickly, thank God), and, of course, I remember my first stylish handbag—a bucket bag that I got when I was eleven (it was red) that had to be part of my life or I would die of shame *(everyone had one)*. How many handbag trends have come and gone since then?

Some accessories are forever and are worth investing in—even saving up for. Others should be bought on a disposable basis. For a list of those worth saving up for, see Chapter 9.

As a general rule, if an item is made by a designer/big-name firm and has been in that line—more or less unchanged—for years, decades, or centuries, this accessory is a classic and is worth buying. That means Chanel logo earrings, Hermès scarf, Louis Vuitton tote bag, etc. If you were wearing all of these items at one time, you would look like a joke—a bad cartoon from *The New Yorker*. But when absorbed into the flow of your entire look, these accents can help define your position to those who look you over.

Shoes

There's this marvelous moment in the movie *Silence of the Lambs* in which Clarice Starling (Jodie Foster) stands in front of the prison cell of Hannibal Lechter (Anthony Hopkins) for the

> *Handbags make the loudest statement about a person's status; but shoes are way up there, too.*

first time, asking him to complete a psychological profile for the FBI. To show his contempt, Lechter says to her, "Do you know what you look like to me with your good bag and your cheap shoes?"

Indeed, cheap shoes are the single worst offense anyone can commit and are the clearest indication anyone has of your financial and social situation. Walk into any grand hotel in the world wearing jeans and a T-shirt— if you're wearing good shoes, you're home free. Go to a job interview in a cheap suit but never in a cheap pair of shoes.

Shoes have become such an important element in a woman's life that some women from Cinderella to Imelda Marcos define their image by the shoes they wear. Think Carmen Miranda and you invariably think of wedgie shoes and a fruited headdress; think Andre Courreges and you think of white vinyl boots. If I say "Birkenstock," you get an immediate profile of the type of person who wears that kind of shoe.

Shoes are one of the few items of clothing that are influenced by fashion and *also* impact on your personal health, well-being, and even safety. Wear a white patent leather handbag before Memorial Day and you'll be cited by the Fashion Police, but that's it. Wear shoes that don't fit properly and you can be temporarily or even permanently crippled.

Please note that fit of a specific pair of shoes can change from wearing to wearing. The shoes stay the same, of course, but variable conditions that change your feet will also affect fit.

Take my rust leather heels—I bought them in Paris during a *crise de pied* (Foot Crisis) when my feet had swelled during a flight and the shoes I brought with me were biting into my flesh, causing tears and agony. The new shoes brought immediate relief. I wore them over town for three days, for about fourteen hours a day, not only for miles of marching but for repeated takes in the filming of a television program that even involved skateboarding in front of the Eiffel Tower in my new shoes.

Fade out Paris and fade in New York, where some months later I pull out the shoes for a day of meetings and appearances that did not involve much walking or stress on the feet. Every step I took that day was murder and after a few blocks, I dashed into a drugstore to buy foot pads. What had happened to the world's most perfect shoes?

My feet were no longer swollen from jet travel and were a smaller size—the shoes rubbed against my shrunken feet, creating blisters, sores, and pain. Poor tootsies! Poor me!

> It's not how good a brand you buy or how chic the shoe is—if it doesn't fit properly, you will suffer.

Feet First

Anyone who's been pregnant, changed body weight, or had a job that requires a lot of standing or walking can tell you that feet certainly do change their size. It's a mistaken assumption to think you will always be the same shoe size, especially as middle age approaches. By age fifty, the incidence of problems with the feet that result in a change in size and shape increase to 70 percent. After all, by the time you are fifty, the average American has walked an average of 75,000 miles. At this point in time, your feet have lost one-half of their natural padding.

Coincidentally, as we get older, we are less likely to tolerate shoes that hurt. The philos-

Cheap Tricks

There are a few cases in life in which I actually recommend cheap shoes, but never for job interviews, status or social events, weddings, or bar mitzvahs. Well, come to think of it, weddings are OK, but only if you are the bride. When to wear cheap shoes?

- Comfort is the most important factor in a shoe, especially in times when you will be putting stress on the feet—therefore, the cost isn't as important as the fit. I have $58 sensible shoes with crepe soles that are far more comfortable for walking all day than any pair of Ferragamos I own. Go for comfort, regardless of price tag. If necessary, adjust your wardrobe around the shoes when your feet will be on duty all day.
- Shoes chosen for a special event, yes, even a wedding, may be most rewarding when they are cheap and virtually disposable; that way you can choose exactly the shoes you need for that one occasion and never feel bad if you don't wear them again. Satin pumps that will be dyed to match, which isn't my idea of true chic but is done all the time, rarely cost more than $50 and can cost a whole lot less—go this route for weird colors, special events, and onetime appearances.
- Cheap shoes are perfect for bad weather wear.
- Cheap shoes are great for a cutting-edge fashion statement—whether it's a pair of spikes or a pair of wedgies, if the shoe style isn't really you but you want to make a fashion statement for a season for just a few outfits, invest in the cheap copy rather than the real thing.
- Do not buy cheap shoes in classic styles (such as simple pumps) and do not buy cheap shoes that are copies of big brands with slight variations—these will always scream "cheap shoes" and harm your image. However, if you have crafty skills, you can buy cheap simple shoes and

add your own embellishments—this is best done with very casual shoes or very dressy shoes and is not for businesswear.

- Cheap shoes can be great for public appearances and dress-up events when you have to look just so, but thankfully for a short period of time that involves no serious walking or dancing. (It's OK to remove shoes to dance.) These shoes can be extreme in that the heel is too high, the toe too pointed, the color too unusual, or whatever—but the shoe works perfectly with a certain outfit or for a certain event. Never invest serious money in a pair of revenge shoes; do spend time searching for just the right cheap pair.

- Sexual impact or innuendo. If I have to explain this, you don't need me to mention it. But yes indeedy, there are shoes that say "catch me if you can" . . . and oh so much more. But you don't need to spend a lot of money on them.

ophy "It's gorgeous; who cares if my feet hurt?" is revised as we get older and wiser. Expect feet to grow longer and wider; you will more than likely be a full size larger at age fifty than you were at age twenty. So listen to your feet when they talk to you, have proper measurements taken, revise your shoe fashion philosophy, and take care of your tootsies so they take care of you.

Sensible Shoes

Buying a big-name/expensive/designer shoe does not guarantee that a shoe will fit. I personally advocate owning many pairs of shoes, not because I suffer from Imelda Marcos Shoe Syndrome, but because I actually like to save my good shoes for special occasions and pick and choose among my shoes depending on weather, situation, and, above all, comfort.

Correlate shoe wearability (and walkability) with price. I

would pay hundreds of dollars for a shoe that looked smart, supported my feet, was comfortable, and allowed me to walk all day without moaning or collapsing. I think the reason brands such as JPTod's, Belgian Loafers, and Ferragamo become cult fixtures is that the shoes will last longer than most brands and seem to support feet. There's also been a movement by athletic shoe companies to move into business and fashion shoes to provide the same support, fit, comfort, and style—check out brands such as Easy Spirit and Rockport.

How well a pair of shoes fits and how long they last relates to:

1. how they are made.
2. how you wear them.

After all, a pair of $500 Manolo Blahniks are quite well made, but they aren't going to hold up if you're joining the cast of Riverdance for their finale or even jogging through the mall on a heavy day's shopping. Remember Michael Johnson, the Olympic athlete who ran in specially made golden shoes and then threw them to the fans in the audience after each run? It wasn't quite the selfless gesture it appeared; the shoes simply wouldn't last for a second go, so they had to go.

Shoes have been worn for thousands of years, and yet it's only until recent history—1858 to be exact—that they were not made by hand. Up until the advent of the machinery that could speed things along, shoes were hand-cut and -sewn; therefore, they were expensive, scarce, hard-won, prized, and meant to last. Some people only had one pair of shoes in a lifetime; the dying often willed their shoes to loved ones. All war movies have bits in them when soldiers are robbed of their boots once fallen on the battlefield or even killed for their shoes.

Nowadays, the average American buys four pairs of shoes a year.

While handmade shoes are superior to machine-made shoes, they are also enormously expensive. A pair of bespoke men's shoes will cost $1,200 to $2,000. Mass-produced shoes range in price from $30 to $300, as an average...but there's a big difference between the two in your wallet. Is there a big difference on your feet?

Shoemaking 101

Since shoes were first created, they have been made of the same basic parts: an upper sewn to a bottom, or sole. Everything else is embroidery...so to speak. When shoes were handmade, they were also custom-sized to the specific foot. Now that they are machine made, there's a range of some three hundred official size and width combinations, from infant 0 to men's 16, with twelve widths ranging from 5A narrow to 4E wide. The average adult shoe is made in four widths.

Shoes are the backbone of every wardrobe and every day's dress-up.

The actual style of the shoe dictates the number of parts it has; the intended retail price dictates the quality of the goods used and many of the mechanical techniques. The introduction of synthetics and all sorts of new technologies after World War II increased the cost-cutting possibilities—you could have shoes made out of fake leather, shoes with rubber soles, or shoes that used glue in places where stitching had once been required.

This is good news for cheap shoes and confusing news for consumers who have to figure out what's what.

Believe it or not, fashion didn't come to the footwear business until the mod, mod, mod years of the 1960s. The industry had begun to change after World War II in response to the new technology, producing a less expensive product, and by the mid to late 1950s the changes in the economics of making shoes were so profound that the industry feared extinction. In order for the shoe business to survive, the public needed to be convinced that shoes

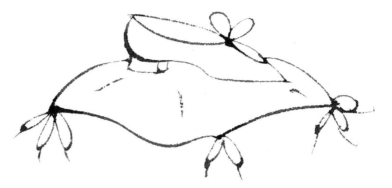

could be regarded as a fashion item, not merely an essential. By the sixties, shoes were part of the fashion picture: the white go-go boots created by Andre Courreges define the whole scene.

The shoe that works is one that has been properly designed to combine technique with creativity. Cinderella's glass slipper may have been a creative masterpiece, but it's short on technological know-how. The shoe designer earns his keep by combining the right materials with the right design for the situation in which the shoe will be worn.

I don't need to tell you that all shoes are not created equal. Because the shoe has a specific job—a burden few other items of clothing have—it must be constructed with an understanding of the conditions in which the shoe will be worn. As I said, those Manolos weren't created for the mall, honey.

A shoe has only two jobs: to both fit and perform well.

When buying shoes, we often lose sight of those facts and instead are seduced by fashion and even sexual statements that the shoes make. Let's face it, what woman hasn't fallen prey to a pair of "fuck me" shoes, caring little about how they fit or performed? A huge portion of the shoes we buy today are chosen for the social statements they make, which is what causes us to lose track of the basics of fit and performance.

Robert Clergerie, a French master of fine—and innovative—shoes, explains that a pair of his shoes goes through some two hundred different operations before they are ready to be shipped out of the factory. His goal in creating his line is to make shoes that look good and fit well—this goal is often lost in less well made shoes. But then, not all feet fit glass slippers.

Just as the marker defines the pattern of a garment, the *last* defines the exact size and shape the shoe manufacturer is working with—and each manufacturer cuts his own last his own way for his own business reasons. For that reason, not all size 7B shoes are identical or will fit the same way. Only bespoke (custom-made) shoes are made on a last that duplicates the wearer's foot.

Even when you find a manufacturer whose last fits you, there is no guarantee that every style from this maker will fit the same way—just as there is no guarantee that the maker will not change the last over time. Since it's rare for both feet to be the same size, the differential in your two feet can very much affect your ability to wear a certain last or even mass-produced shoes.

Traditionally, shoes are made from leather, and that leather normally comes from the hides of animals that are eaten for food, though you will encounter shoes made from the hides of horse and reptiles as well. The type of hide used for the shoe very much affects the way the shoe fits.

Even though very few shoes are handmade, even those that are touted as handmade, such as JPTod's, may be only partially hand-assembled; frequently these shoes are stitched by a machine to *look* as if they were hand-stitched. Don't pay handmade prices unless you're certain actual hands worked on the shoes. Machine stitching is so sophisticated these days that you've got everything from the Goodyear welt, which looks like hand-stitching, to Mock Goodyear, which is actually ornamental—they use glue.

The flexibility of the leather relates to how comfortable a shoe will be, especially since the foot expands during the day. Hand-

Who's Who in the Shoe Zoo

Buckskin: Davy Crockett would be proud—deerskin or elkskin used mostly in moccasins or saddle shoes; it's sturdy.

Buffalo: This is water buffalo, not American bison, Ms. Oakley; heavy and sturdy with very little give.

Calfskin: The veal of shoe leathers, calfskin comes from animals that ranged in age from days old to months old before they met the great cow in the sky. The skins weigh up to fifteen pounds; the leather is fine-grained, lightweight, much more supple than cowhide, and makes the best handbags and shoes.

Cordovan: Made from horse rumps; nonporous and very durable; used more in men's shoes than women's because it's so stiff.

Cowhide: Git along li'l doggies—the most commonly used leather for shoes because it's tough and it lasts. It can be made more supple by being layered or cut very thinly, but this leather is not usually chosen for pliability.

Kangaroo: Tie me kangaroo down, boys, this is one of the strongest of all leathers, resembling glazed kid with a finer grain.

Kid: Baby goatskin; it's very porous and allows a good bit of air to reach the foot, but it's a bit fragile.

Kip: Mid-aged, midsized cow, between a calf and a cow, sturdy.

Lamb: Lambskin and sheepskin are indistinguishable after tanning—both are very flexible.

Pig: Moi? Miss Piggy offers surface texture with a pimply dotted design (think football) but is rarely used in shoes.

Shark: Reverses the dog-eat-dog rule; it's tough and it's water-repellent, but be careful: its distinctive texture can be faked with embossing—rarely used in shoes but sometimes seen in boots.

Snake: Decorative but not very sturdy.

stitching also makes for a more comfortable shoe, as it moves with the leather and has slightly more give, allowing the shoe to better conform itself to the foot as the foot moves.

The "breaking in" process with a new pair of shoes means that the materials soften to frame the foot and yield at the pressure points. But don't count on all shoes to contour themselves to your foot—their ability to ease is related to how they were made and what leathers were used. Synthetics cannot be "broken in"; suede has the most give to it. Leather also breathes, whereas plastic and synthetics do not; a breathing entity can react to foot perspiration and expansion far more comfortably than a rigid shoe.

Choose the shoes you wear each day based on the demands of the day and how much walking you will do.

Though you should never buy an uncomfortable pair of shoes, if you do find your shoes are pinching, you can stretch them by putting them in the freezer with a baggie filled with water set into each foot. As the water freezes, it expands, stretching the shoe. The freezing temperature also constricts the leather, molding it to this new shape. (This does not work with man-made materials.)

Fit

A shoe's fit depends on the circumstances in which the shoe is worn and whether or not those circumstances will cause your feet to sweat, swell, or whatever. The lining material of the shoes affects the fit, as does the breathability and absorption of the uppers and the insoles. The height of the heel will affect not only fit but comfort. Remember:

- Measure your feet in the Brannock device while you are standing up!
- Wear the proper hosiery, as thickness of hosiery will affect fit. If

you are trying on boots that will be worn with socks, have socks with you.

- Not only are your two feet probably different sizes, but there are life forces that can change the shape and size of your feet, including pregnancy, weight gain, and weight loss. Long hours of standing affect the size and shape of your feet, as well as how the shoes will wear, as do different styles of walking. In short, the way the shoe fits is related to the specific movements of the feet inside the shoes.

Try on shoes at the end of the day, not the beginning, because your feet swell as the day progresses.

Heels

Naturally it was the French who invented the high heel. Before the sixteenth century, shoes were flat. Heels were first introduced for court shoes and for the military; within fifty years, all shoes had heels.

Heels are most often made of wood but can be anything from wadded-up leftover leather to rubber or steel or even gold. The rubber heel was introduced in 1896 as a comfort measure and is still the most popular heel for a flat shoe.

Men's shoes tend to have a solid rubber heel, although nylon is sometimes used. Women's heels are either wooden or injected plastic. A crepe heel is the most comfortable; most durable is leather; least comfortable is plastic.

While women's heels can vary in height from one to four inches, most medical professionals agree that no one should wear a heel that is higher than two and a half inches. For comfort, the optimal heel height is between one inch and one and a half inches.

The width of the heel is also important, as the wider the heel is, the better it distributes your weight. Wedges are therefore the best, and stilettos are the worst (but you knew that). Some heels have a wide neck and then taper to a tiny shape; since the width of the base helps distribute the wearer's weight, this style is preferable to a straight drop in a narrow heel. The Sabrina heel is a good example of this effect.

The Multiple-Shoe Theory

Call me irresponsible, but I believe in having similar shoes for different purposes in life. You've just read about the numerous factors that affect fit; you've seen my great belief in cheap shoes under certain conditions (see pages 166–167). My lifestyle places me in so many different situations that I need a wardrobe of shoes with just as much variety. I also like to nurse my investment in my expensive shoes, to make them last as many years as possible.

The most important shoe in my basic wardrobe is a dress-up shoe with a low heel that can go everywhere. In my case, I depend on the Ferragamo shoe called Tuxedo, a one-inch-heel shoe with a grosgrain ribbon bow on the front, and a few pairs of low-heeled Manolos. But these shoes are very expensive, and I nurse them, saving them for times when I really need them. When they get worn out or ruined by snow, rain, sleet, or hail, I still keep them, cherish them, and designate them my bad-weather shoes. Furthermore, when the sale comes along, I may buy two of the same or similar shoes, especially if they're an unusual color. Like most big-name firms, Ferragamo does a group of colors every season that probably will not be repeated any time in the near future. God knows, every season I pray for a new olive green suede shoe.

Sooo, when I find that a strange color is successful for me, I stock up during the sale, or if I happen on the shoe at any of my bargain resources. However, I also stock up on basics…when the price is right. I just bought a new pair of the Tuxedo shoe in black leather that I didn't need at all, but it was on sale at a bargain store

Metric Heels

I was trying on shoes in Saks and thought the heel seemed a tad high. I asked the salesman if it was an unusual height. "Oh no, it's the usual four centimeters," he assured me. Metric in America? Yep. Furthermore, the standard European heel heights do not correlate directly to American inches. (To convert, note that 1 inch equals about 2.5 centimeters.) Here are the most commonly encountered heel heights:

11 cm = 4⅜ inches
   Rarely found, about as high as they go.
10 cm = 4 inches
   This is the average height for a very high heel or stiletto.
9 cm = 3½ inches
   This is a common height for a high shoe.
8 cm = 3¼ inches
   Believe it or not, the French consider this a medium heel.
5 cm = 2 inches
   Higher but still considered medium.
4 cm = 1½ inches, and a hair
   A low heel by French standards; medium in America.
3 cm = 1¼ inches
   This is a low heel.

for $55 (OK, it was $69 but I had a coupon that made it $55), and for $55 how could I pass it by?

OK, so now you have some of the basics about the classical part of a good shoe wardrobe, but that is just the backbone. I also have a selection of fashion heels for dinner out, dress-up, public appearances, or look-sees. I cannot walk diddly-squat in them and cannot keep them on my feet for more than a few hours at a time, but they make the outfit, and at a good price, they thrill me.

I also have a wardrobe of rainy-day shoes, once-expensive shoes already ruined by the elements, or fabulously comfortable shoes that cost so little that I can risk losing them.

A shoe wardrobe can be broken down into many compartments, with one pair of shoes in the same color in each compartment:

DRESS-UP	BUSINESS
WALK ALL DAY	BAD WEATHER

Finding Shoe Bargains

It's certainly no challenge to spend $200 or more on a single pair of shoes, though one can spend far less and get perfectly serviceable shoes—especially if you have access to a good off-price or outlet store. And it's not always easy to see what accounts for the differential between costly shoes and lower-priced footwear.

Several years ago I discovered a brand of shoes called Aerosoles; they have their own stores and mail-order operation but also have department store distribution. I happened to find them in their freestanding store at Mall of America and had never heard of the line before I wandered in. As someone who had been paying $150 a pair for most of her shoes, I found Aerosoles' regular retail prices of about $35 to $55 per pair of shoes to be, well, refreshing. Once I also found out they were great on my feet, I became a serial buyer. So I go to New Orleans on a business trip and luck into an Aerosoles shop and I find a great new style at $55 a pair and buy three pairs in different colors. I am thrilled with my purchase—basically three pairs for the cost of one pair of Ferragamos.

I was somewhat less thrilled the next week when I saw what appeared to be the exact same shoe for $34 a pair at a discount store in New York. At first I thought they were my shoes but marked down. When I read the box, however, I saw that they were similar models in a lower-priced line made by the same company. Like many brands, Aerosoles makes product to be sold at different price points; obviously you're getting some differences in quality. Line extensions, bridge lines, and diffusion lines are popular marketing tricks in garments and now in shoes. Often the fit is the same, just the quality of the workmanship is different.

Unusual Sizes

Whether you wear a size 5 or a size 11, if you need an odd-sized shoe you should be mindful of a few shopping rules:

- If you need something, buy it early in the season, as the store may indeed get only one pair in your size.
- When you find a last or a firm or a shoe that really works for you, stock up even if it means buying two pairs of the same shoe—you just never know when you'll get this lucky again.
- If you have big feet, try men's shoes—especially for casual shoes. If you have small feet, try the children's department (a girls' size 3½ is equivalent to a woman's size 5).

- Find a good shoe repair shop and really take care of your shoes. Well-fitting shoes have to be treated with the same respect as a friend.
- Find a company that copies shoes so that if you've got a wonderful pair that needs replacing, you can have a duplicate pair made to measure. (Look in the Yellow Pages under shoemaker.)

Handbags

How does a salesperson in a fancy store know how to treat you—how can they tell if you are a looky-lou or a serious shopper and what makes them be nice to you or take you seriously?

The quality of your handbag. That's it, that's the whole answer. How you are treated in a store, and many other aspects of service businesses, is directly related to how expensive your handbag is.

In fact, did you know that the Queen of England carries an empty handbag? Do you mind if I digress here, it's rather fascinating…you see, as Queen, it's uh, demeaning for her to handle money—someone follows after her to take care of the real-people part of it. So why does she carry a handbag if it's empty? I thought you'd never ask! Because it's used for a signal device to her staff—note that all the Queen's handbags are constructed the same way and all have short straps held on her wrist—no shoulder bags for Ma'am. She turns the bag at different angles and directions to signal her staff in how to rescue her from specific situations. Honest, I could not make this up.

Unless you are the Queen of England, you need a handbag. To a salesperson (or a hotelier), the bag itself—from the outside only—says exactly who you are. You can wear jeans, running shoes, and no socks, but if you have the right handbag, you're in. The three giveaways to a person's status, all checked within seconds in one swift glance, are, in this order: handbag, shoes, watch.

When I was growing up, a woman matched her handbag to her shoes. That is now considered extremely déclassé. Most women now have a small wardrobe of bags devoted to everyday use based on the seasons, as it's way too time-consuming to change handbags on a daily basis. With more wear attached to any given bag, the perimeters of price and need change as one can afford to make more of an investment and more of a statement.

Many of my theories about shoes apply to handbags as well. I have more than one handbag in the same color, each at a different price point and in different stages of wear so that I can baby my good bags, saving them for impact value.

I recently invested $400 (and that was the sale price!) in a handbag for travel because it was so expensive-looking (it originally sold for almost $1,000) and the salesman at the designer shop where I bought it swore it was indestructible. If this bag takes the stress of travel off my wardrobe of good bags, then it's a sensible investment. This is an alternate investment strategy.

In addition to all these fancy handbags, I have regular bags that are used for real life, each of which costs less than $50. I also have a series of baskets and tote bags that coordinate with them because I carry so much junk with me during the day.

Keeping your bag and tote coordinated gives you a more polished look. I've seen many businesswomen, for example, who use two Coach bags—this seems to be a very popular trend that keeps the look coordinated and simple. I happen to prefer a mixed-texture look and think the tote bag can be less serious (and less expensive) than the handbag.

Bag Basics

Handbags are made of all sorts of materials and vary in shape from the simple envelope clutch to elaborate contraptions constructed by architects or engineers. How well a bag lasts and wears is directly related to the construction of the bag, what you put in it, and how the materials wear under the stress of the contents and real-life knocking about.

Forget "you are what you eat." In public, you are your handbag.

Any handbag will wear well if you carry only a lipstick and a credit card in it and trot it out just for the dinner hours. Bags that go in and out of cars, trains, planes, buses, rain, elevators, crowds, and real life are not going to fare as well. Save investment bags for important meetings and appearances when a handbag makes a statement.

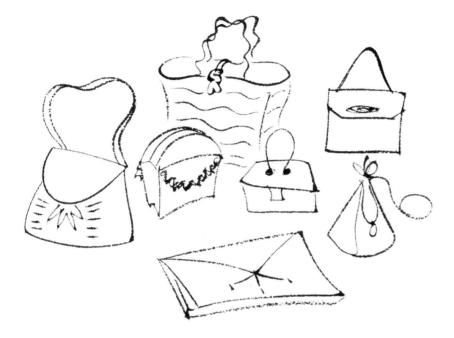

A heavily constructed handbag has the best shot at a long life—look at the Kelly bag—but may not be that easy to get in and out of. An unconstructed bag relies on the strength of the leather it is made of in order to hold up and also presents the problem of the bottomless pit—who can find anything in a large hobo bag? Carrying a lot of clutter in your bag can damage the shape of the bag and your back and/or shoulders.

Bag Bodies

Since a handbag can have three parts or thirty parts, it's hard to talk comparative anatomy here. But it is well worth knowing which elements are most likely to show stress and wear, which indicate a bag of good quality, and where you can cheat the eye.

Frame: The metal structure over which the leather or other handbag material is stretched. Naturally this implies a constructed bag, such as the Kelly or the Bolide. Most modern handbags do not have a frame and have a more relaxed structure and silhouette.

Gussets: These side panels make the fold (like an envelope fold) that allows a bag to expand when you fill it. Again, it's a more old-fashioned notion for a constructed bag, but my new Ferragamo bag has gussets. Note that gussets can come in accordion format to provide more room and compartments inside a bag—this is seen most often in evening bags or ladies-who-lunch handbags.

Handles and Straps: Retro and vintage bags have handles, as do many newer bags. Handles need to carry the weight of what's in the bag and work with your own body and your lifestyle.

Closures and Hardware: Handbags can be opened and closed by any number of devices, anything from a drawstring, which is a nonmetallic part, to snaps, to any sort of clasp, including magnetic clasps. Hardware can range from D-rings on a strap to signature bits used by Gucci or even the little brass feet on the bottom of many constructed handbags. It is the quality of the hardware that often tells how expensive the bag is; hardware is often engraved with the name and/or logo of the designer or manufacturer.

Buy inexpensive handbags for the style statement they make and enjoy them in everyday life or on weekends or for casual travel. This lengthens the life span of your expensive bags.

For example, the hardware of all Hermès bags says Hermès… which is why the really chic way to wear your Kelly bag is with part of the buckle fastened and one strap undone so that it falls away to reveal the word *Hermès* engraved on the closure.

Ornamentation: Anything from trim to novelties added to the design or logo. This includes signature touches, which often replace a formal logo. Gucci's famous red-and-green-striped ribbon is a good example, as well as Paloma Picasso's 'x' kisses.

How to Buy a Bag

A bag that you love and that lasts twenty years is indeed well worth $500, if you stick to the rules and use it all those years.

Don't rationalize yourself into a rash purchase, but don't waste $50 a year for ten years either.

Stitching should be small and even, no hanging strings. Take a good sniff—real leather smells like real leather and goat actually *smells* cheaper than lamb—the more you sniff, the more clearly you'll see the difference. Once you've touched the lambskin sides of a real Chanel handbag you will know why they cost so much.

Different kinds of leather go in and out of fashion—right now highly polished calf is considered very chic. I have two expensive bags made in this style—both scratched early on and left me sick. There indeed seems to be some correlation between high style, high price, and high maintenance. (Fill in scratches with matching felt-tipped marker.) You're always safer with leather that has some texture to it that can hide scratches—or even something like alligator (this is just an example—don't panic) or alligator-stamped cowhide—and so much surface interest that you don't notice daily wear and tear as much.

Before you buy a handbag, or even begin your search, ask yourself questions that require honest answers: Are you looking for a status bag? A sensible bag? A cheap thrill? How much wear and stress will the bag take? Will it be used daily or only when a big impression is your goal? How long is it expected to last in your wardrobe? Play fair with yourself so that you have reasonable expectations of your purchase.

Classic bags are worth a significant financial investment—but only if they are built to last; when created in fragile hides like lambskin they should be considered solely as status symbols. Weird bags bought on sale that go with a zillion things and class up the simplest clothes are often worth the madness attached to such a purchase—but never pay full price.

Consider man-made fibers and plastics for either the practical touch they add (look what Prada did with nylon!) or for the fun statement they can make. Many status lines have PVC (plastic)

outershells—Louis Vuitton, one of the most sought-after brands, made a fortune selling plastic-coated canvas.

Don't limit your scrutiny to the outside of the bag—look at the lining and exactly how well made that lining may or may not be. The inside of a bag is a better giveaway to the bag's true worth than the outside. Also check the maker's signature touches. Some have logos; some offer guarantees or company histories; some are stamped with specific information. For example, a real Chanel bag usually says "Made in Italy" inside it (not "Made in France").

Even if you are looking at a casual summer bag—perhaps one that is basketlike in style—if it's expensive, it still should be lined. How well lined it is and whether or not the lining has pockets that zip are all indications of quality that will affect the price. How well zippers and all closures work is paramount in judging the value of a bag.

When examining how the straps or handles are attached, look at a lot of quality bags to get an education in physics and engineering. Sure, a leather strap can be stitched or double-stitched to the bag and look like it's got support, but zigzag and x-cross stitching inside a square of topstitching give even more support.

It's important not to be too influenced by the designer name on a bag but instead to go for the values of workmanship and craftsmanship—combined with a good notion of what makes sense for you. Do you carry three pairs of eyeglasses with you in your every-day bag? Then a tiny little flower-basket confection, no matter how chic and how endearing, is not going to make much sense, is it? (Drat.) If, on the other hand, you tend to be a pack rat, a capacious bucket-style bag may encourage you to carry your life on your shoulder, while a trimmer envelope style would force you to edit and limit your load.

Your Handbag Wardrobe

If you don't want to buy as many bags as I do, try to pick a basic bag that works with a lot of things and possibly team it with a tote so that the tote takes the stress and carries the bulkier items that could ruin a good bag or disallow a small bag. A small bag packed

Weird Handbag Science

While I'm a big believer in basics and classics for the long run, if you have limited choices in your handbag wardrobe I think that the opposite theories of Weird Jacket Science should be considered (see pages 108–109). My point is that one strange shade in a bag can be used more effectively than one classic bag. While this may seem counterintuitive, handbags in unexpected (yet soft) colors can be even more versatile than a muted brown or safe black bag, and add a lot more pizzazz to your look.

Strange colors give you the opportunity to make a fashion statement, broaden your look, stick to one handbag for most days, and express some individuality. I have a dark green bag for winter and a cornflower blue bag for spring-summer. I wear them with all colors except black and red, and they are my regular bags (if I'm wearing black I'll switch to black, if I'm wearing red I'll switch to burgundy). My newest handbag is one I purchased from the Coach Company Store in a soft apple green shade. I've gone from boring to bold in one purchase.

Bagging a Look

If you don't want to go the designer route, you can get creative and inventive with many types of products and turn them into chic handbags just by being witty. For years I have used a tin lunch box from the 1950s as a handbag. I bought it at a flea market for $10. I've also seen women use fishing baskets, tackle boxes, and all sorts of vintage pieces of fabrics. A handbag is one of the few areas where you can get creative so that people can see you have style with a twist.

with essentials and a large tote with other essentials can work to save you money and make a style statement at the same time.

If you want a wardrobe of limited basics, therefore, I suggest:

- two bags of high quality in unusual colors, one for spring and one for fall
- one black handbag
- one evening bag, preferably a neutral color and seasonless in style—avoid velvets
- totes or baskets that coordinate (but don't necessarily match) with each day bag

The best way to judge the quality of a handbag is to touch it, smell it, and eyeball the insides as well as the outsides.

Should you be able to expand the wardrobe, I'd broaden it with a group of classic handbags in basic colors: brown, navy, burgundy, beige. I mix white and beige all the time and see no reason why you have to own a white bag.

If you want to expand your evening bag collection, have a black evening bag and then a multicolor funky job that goes with many things. Try to avoid cheapie evening bags. Even though you won't use your evening bags often, they can bring down your ensemble for the evening in a matter of seconds. No evening bag at all is better than a cheap-looking evening bag.

Faking It

Of all the areas of fake goods, I think the most popular is the fake designer handbag. If you are tempted to buy a fake because you don't want to sacrifice a big chunk of your fashion wardrobe on one oft-copied item, I remind you that while, yes, some people can get away with it, for the most part, fakes undermine your look and are an act of self-loathing on your part. Buy the best bag you can afford or save up for a good bag bought on sale, but don't fall for a fake. End of speech.

In the eyes of those who spot your fake designer handbag for what it is, you are forever diminished.

Well, maybe not end of speech. There is a world of difference between fakes and copies, although it is often hard to determine when a copy becomes a fake and when it is merely inspired by a very costly original and a legitimate purchase in its own right. Just about every major handbag house has a version of the Kelly bag, the quilted Chanel bag, even the newer Gucci Hobo bag. An inspiration is fine as long as there is no attempt to copy the logo features of the original.

When I see a handbag with a bamboo handle that was inspired by the Gucci style I wince if the bamboo is too thin and spindly—it gives the bag's inferior provenance away in a flash. When I see a

fake Prada bag on the street, I think less of the stranger who carries it. I'm not the only one who feels that way.

Since there are lots of alternative shopping venues, from big clearance sales at department stores to factory outlets that offer good-quality pieces at essentially the same price you would pay for a fake or a bad copy that's handily bought, I recommend holding out for the real thing. There is glory in denying yourself the instant gratification of a quick fix and waiting for the opportunity to score on quality. And don't discount the confidence that walking into a chic restaurant with an unimpeachable correct symbol of success on your arm will give you.

Scarves, Shawls, and Wraps

It's often been said that all one really needs to own is one black skirt and two white blouses and a drawer full of Hermès scarves. I hate people who can embark on a weeklong trip with little more in their carry-on than one black suit and a lot of scarves. And yet we've all met someone with this facility (and confidence) and know this is one of the best magic acts in history.

Pashmina and Shahtush

If you read a lot of society columns, or study the fine print in British fashion magazines, you are already onto the fact that for the last few years the ultimate in luxury has been a giant scarf, worn as a shawl, made of a fiber called *pashmina*. These precious wraps, made from the hair of a goat, cost anywhere from $500 to $1,000 per.

You don't get it? No problem.

In the last decade of luxury, where less is more and more is less (this is a philosophy, not a puzzle), everyone knows to travel with a cashmere shawl because it's comforting on an emotional level and practical in that you never know when you'll get chilly on a flight or in your hotel suite. Alas, a cashmere shawl can be bulky and inconvenient when you're traveling through different weather zones.

Enter pashmina, as soft and as warm as cashmere, and even more luxurious, so fine that you can draw its bulk through a ring (which is why they are sometimes called Ring Scarves). For the cherry on top of this morsel, note that the fiber dyes incredibly well so that all sorts of yummy colors can be achieved (which means you must have more than one!).

Indeed, those in the know eschew black, brown, or navy and go for something wild and weird and very sophisticated, the theory being the more you have, in the more wild and weird shades, the better your wealth and status are defined. Pashmina shawls are sold only at exclusive boutiques like Barneys in the United States, but in London they are easier to find and also come in prints (usually Indian or paisley) or with embroidery. There's also a wider range in price differences in London, where you can get in for as little as $200 (at Portobello market for £125).

Even more exclusively (and four times as costly) are *shahtush* shawls. Shahtush shawls are cousins of pashmina shawls. Woven from the softest little hairballs this side of Tibet, shahtush is rendered from an antelope, not a goat. Since antelopes are on the endangered species list, trade in shahtush anything is illegal in Europe, India, and the United States. Both pashmina and shahtush shed.

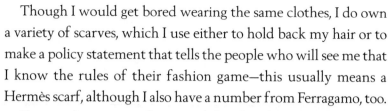

Though I would get bored wearing the same clothes, I do own a variety of scarves, which I use either to hold back my hair or to make a policy statement that tells the people who will see me that I know the rules of their fashion game—this usually means a Hermès scarf, although I also have a number from Ferragamo, too.

To me, a designer scarf is a social shorthand. I try to use mine in witty or creative ways—in my hair, as mentioned, or tied to a handbag or even through the belt loops of a pair of jeans. If I do tie a scarf around my neck, I invariably use a man's tie knot rather than following any of the instructions in those "tie your scarf in a million ways" booklets.

Shawls

Though not a wardrobe in itself, a scarf or its oversized cousin the shawl is a grand accessory.

- Spend some time in the bedding department of department and discount stores to find a piano throw or a small blanket that makes a divine wrap.
  - Airline blankets make excellent shawls.
  - Bedspreads or curtains can do as a wrap, especially if they are silky, crinkly, or textured. Think Scarlett O'Hara.
  - I read this idea in a magazine, so I can't take credit for it. If you're going out on the town for a winter evening and are worried about freezing to death but don't want to buy an expensive wrap, buy a piece of Thinsulate and some fancy fabric, perhaps a velvet and a chiffon or moire, and then make a giant square (or oblong stole) lined with the Thinsulate to serve as a shawl. It will be lightweight (and provide excellent drape) but will be warm because of the inner lining.

Artificial Flowers

I have no doubt that artificial flowers came into vogue as a substitute for jewelry; surely our beloved Coco Chanel had something to do with this. Both Chanel suits, and later, Adolfo suits, are finished off with a matching or coordinating camellia worn at the neck or on the shoulder. St. John also claims the camellia as its flower and uses a camellia on many of its suits. No other jewelry is required. The grace and understatement of the flower adds a polish that would make diamonds seem downright inappropriate.

Other types of flowers besides camellias have also become acceptable on suits, so that you can now wear a small portion of the Chelsea Flower Show and pass on owning gold, silver, or any other type of accessory. Naturally, your *faux fleur* is *faux,* usually silk, but not always—I've seen everything from linen to patent leather. I'm partial to velvet myself.

Each season you can walk into the first-floor accessories department of any major department store to look at tray after tray of flowers attached to pinbacks priced from $25 on up, way up—the good ones are often over $50. Of course, at Chanel, they cost *much* more ($150 to $250).

So I go to my nearby craft store and buy a bloom by the stalk, priced anywhere from $4.99 to $7.99. Then I snap off the stem

Bonnie's Coat Trick

My friend Bonnie lives in Beverly Hills, where they wear real Chanel and no one would dare be caught dead with a fake. Bonnie bought a plain, simple black wool coat at a discount store and a real Chanel flower, which she wore on the collar. Instant chic. Constant pleasure. Reasonable total cash outlay.

with wire cutters. I used to turn them into a proper pin, binding the edge and attaching it to a pinback with tape. But, I had a lot of trouble getting the pins to hang properly on the garment. I quit adding the pinback and now I just buy a multipack of hatpins and affix them directly to my garment.

I keep most of my flowers attached to the blouse or suit jacket they have been coordinated with for two reasons: (1) it saves me time scrambling to find the right color flower and (2) it saves on the wear and tear of the fabric as every time you stick a pin into fabric, you make holes.

chapter 8

Trendspotting and Fashion-Mongering

Wardrobe Extension

after you've built your basic wardrobe, you aren't done. *You're never done!* Sit back for too long, neglect the wardrobe, and it will grow stale on you, throwing you into panic when a few years down the line you realize you really do have a closet filled with clothes and nothing to wear. Worse, you can fall into a personality rut because there's been so little input into your message that you just become a watered-down version of yourself. If you are alive, your wardrobe should be alive.

These are the areas where you can always add on to freshen up your look:

- Buy an inexpensive yet trendy pair of shoes to update a classic suit.
- Buy trousers in the newest silhouette to team with existing blazers.
- Buy disposable chic to update a suit or take it from day to night. Shells, camisoles, and chic T-shirts that reflect a trend but aren't too expensive are worth buying, especially at the beginning of a trend. Remember lace T-shirts? Well, even if you don't, it makes my point. When they were "in," they were hot—they were the beginning of the lingerie look, actually. Then the lingerie look got a lot more explicit and lace T-shirts were stupid. But for two years and $16 each they were worth a small investment.

- Buy a shape or style in a cheapie version to try it out yet enjoy the trend.
- Buy anything black that you love that will expand your basic black wardrobe and add a kicky touch that gives it more zip. However, don't buy it because it matches—buy it because you love it and it breathes new energy into a wardrobe that can get stale and boring quickly.

To Trend or Not to Trend

Fashion is ephemeral; it changes with the seasons and the moods of man. Style is classic; it is forever. Trends are merely a small part of the fashion business. You should feel confident enough to take 'em or leave 'em. But if you had to rate trends on a thrill basis, they provide a high that few of us can resist.

Frankly, I think that adapting a few items off the trend smorgasbord makes you feel more with it; picking a few trendy items is a nice way to move your wardrobe forward, even if you end up discarding those when they become obsolete. My perspective is probably based on the fact that I am in an aspect of the fashion business—I like fashion. For many people, trends are waste of time…and money.

Trends are the way we get our energy. Most of us need the energy a new item imparts far more than we actually need the item itself.

If the point of fashion and style and seasonal clothing updates is to offer you the chance to renew yourself each morning when you dress and to re-create yourself each time you dress for a special event, then trends—the backbone of fashion and the antithesis of style—are an important part of the mix. Trends keep me young, they make me laugh, they are part of the seduction of fashion. OK, so I'm a cheap date. Sue me. And take my square-toed pink satin pilgrim shoes, will you?

Every collection a designer offers to the public is brought forth with one basic underlying psychology: the human need to reinvent ourselves. Yes, trends are often about selling you something you don't need (or a new version of something you already have), but *there is a psychological need here that relates to renewal.* The energy that comes from renewal knows no season; clothes are about capturing that energy and carrying it forward.

Some people are immune to trends. Those with classic personal style or those with their own signature style rarely succumb to trends. Most of us fall in the deep water in between—we are tempted by trends but don't want to look foolish or like a fashion victim who meekly follows the crowd. More important, we don't want to throw good money after bad trends.

Trendiness Is Next to Godliness

Where do trends start and how do you know which ones to latch onto? Are you willing to invest in some trends as long as you get them on the upswing rather than the downswing? Do you feel left out or in the dark when a trend begins and find yourself impressed by it only as it goes commercial and threatens to become cheap or common?

We have ways to make you trendy.

Trends are spawned in two completely different camps:

1. the couture
2. the street

The Street: Much couture is influenced by the street, so diehards might say that *all* trends begin in the streets. I disagree. However, if a trend makes it from the street to couture, it has to have legs.

There are professional trendspotters who hang out with teenagers and go to clubs and concerts and high schools and malls and speak teen-speak and can predict where this market is going far enough in advance to develop product for this segment of the

Evolution of a Trend

Although we seem to see trends in stores and fashion magazines at the same time, many of them creep up more slowly, working their way from teen and street culture. Trends are evolutionary, not revolutionary. Take a look at the timing in this recent trend.

- My son throws out all his normal blue jeans and buys new jeans three sizes larger, which he wears low and baggy.
- Six months later, he throws out all those new jeans because he "needs" new jeans, these with cargo pocket and also worn low, big, and baggy.
- Six months later, I read in the trade newspaper *Women's Wear Daily* that this trend for baggy jeans—cargo jeans, thank you—has carried into mass-produced jeans.
- Six months later, I begin to see said look in cargo jeans, trousers, and even skirts.
- Six months later, Karl Lagerfeld shows a soft, wide-leg, droopy trouser suit at a Chanel couture runway show. Street has slowly been absorbed into couture and will affect the silhouette of millions of garments. Time elapsed = two and a half years.

population. To them, all inspiration comes from the street because the street runs two to three years ahead of the catwalk; this gives spotters time to watch for a while before they decide to hop onto it and take it one step closer to mass marketing.

The amount of time it takes for a street trend to travel gives the smart shopper time to spot, modify, and adjust without being silly…and without constantly investing money in looks that will be a flash in the fashion frying pan.

Couture: Once Lagerfeld has shown it, I know we have a done deal. I make a point to stop buying cigarette-leg jeans or capri-style pants. I have seen the handwriting on the wall. I know the change will happen within a season or two. I order a trouser suit with baggy pants from my tailor in Hong Kong. Because I am ahead of my time, I know that this suit will last me two or three years and will be (a) a mistake or (b) a pivotal point in the next digression of my wardrobe. Stay tuned.

Where to Spot Trends

The single best way to stay on top of trends is to read *Women's Wear Daily*, the most influential trade publication for fashion.

You must not only study the pictures of what's coming out but read the articles and all but memorize the fabric reports. The future trends are all predicted in the fabric reports, because all fashion is shaped by fabric first. Likewise, by knowing who is cutting what fabrics, you can judge the crest of a trend.

Maximize your fashion buys and watch trends develop by reading trade papers like *Women's Wear Daily*. A one-year subscription is pricey ($200), but you will save much more than that by knowing what styles to buy early and when to stop buying others. For subscription information call 800-289-0273.

Another keen choice is to go to nightclubs, especially in fashion capitals. Don't go to yuppie clubs, go to cutting-edge clubs where there's lots of kids and funky people who make up their own looks to get noticed—from their ideas, a trend will sprout.

Make rounds of vintage clothing stores and casually ask what's been selling, what trends they see, who's been buying what. I latched onto the fur-trimmed-collar three-quarter-length-sleeve jacket ($32) when the salesgirl at a vintage clothing store in New York (Screaming Mimi) told me that Miu Miu Prada, and several supermodels had all bought similar jackets in the last two weeks. Lemminglike, I suddenly had to have one.

Spy on celebs, even if it means browsing the tabs while at the checkout counter of the grocery store. Don't read the stories, just look at the pictures, especially from awards ceremonies, where celebs turn out in all sorts of things—from biker pants with a ball gown (Demi Moore) to sneakers with sequins (Cybil Shepherd)—but you also see the next trends: Nicole Kidman in Dior chinoiserie.

Smart shoppers have one eye on the teenagers at the mall and another on the couture shows in Paris and Milan.

Trend Prowling

To be on top of the next trends, yet to coordinate your existing wardrobe and library of clothes with this look, you need some regular sources of information and inspiration. Try this ritual:

- Read *Women's Wear Daily,* the trade newspaper of the garment industry in America. It's printed five days a week and covers every aspect of fashion, so you will get everything you need from fabrics to fashion.
- Read American fashion magazines, especially *In-Style, Marie Claire,* and *Elle,* which really tell you how to get a look; read *Vogue* and *Harper's Bazaar* for trends and styles.
- Study British, French, and Italian fashion magazines for greater inspiration. You don't have to be able to read the language, just look at the pictures. If your library doesn't carry them, go to a hairdresser who subscribes and browse—Euro trends often inspire U.S. trends, so you can get an early glimpse of the future.
- Go shopping in your closet (see pages 113–115) for clothes and accessories that you've "retired" that mimic trends you've seen in the magazines.
- Visit a good consignment shop or two and some vintage clothing stores to see what you can fill in at a fair price that is "coming back again" and covers a new trend or style.
- Window-shop the really expensive collections to see what ideas you can steal or copy or make or modify from your existing wardrobe.
- Shop what I call "teenage stores," which are the first to jump on a hot trend and copy it, producing it at an affordable price (even if with lower-quality goods). My regulars include Contempo and Strawberry, which are both chains.

You can always see where a trend is going and when it will end by watching the fabrications reports in the trade papers.

I should also tell you that transparent fabrics and lace-edged underwear looks should be working their way out of style; I know for a fact that they are nearly over—every fiber in my body says so. I know to stop investing in these styles now and to wear what I already own while they are "hot." Yet the lace trim marches on for another year.

Surely there will be a great closet in the sky where we can park all our investments of the moment—I will personally donate my lace T-shirts, my Diane Freis dresses (although I smell a comeback here), anything with ruffles, my broomstick skirts, my stirrup stretch pants, and all my shoulder pads. I write this as I make room in my closet for this little cardigan sweater trimmed in marabou feathers that is just so cute that I couldn't resist....

Trend Calendar

Couture shows are held in Paris twice a year. Spring fashions are shown in January; fall is shown in July. Ready-to-wear shows are also held twice a year. Fall is shown in March, and spring is shown in October. These are the two most influential sets of shows in the manufacturing end of a trend.

From when you see a photograph in March—of a look that will be available in the upcoming fall—you have approximately seven months (maybe more) to get ready. This is ample time to sew some things on your own or to begin looking for affordable versions of the concepts you've seen shown...to go shopping in your attic, to start thinking in new directions and modifying your shopping habits or limiting your purchases.

This time frame clearly tells you what to stop buying. If the fabrics featured in the new collections don't look like anything you already own, cease buying existing styles

It's always better to get out of a trend early than to get into one late.

immediately and hold out for the new look. Tweed is coming. Count on it.

On the average, the life cycle of a trend is about three years. Once the look is available at Kmart or Wal-Mart you know it's at the end of its run. But nowadays technology allows knock-off houses to get in on a trend much more quickly than in the past, which may give that trend greater endurance.

I do not claim to have a crystal ball for picking which trends will have the legs to become classics and which will die, or even which ones will die quickly. Sure I knew not to get into pouf dresses. But I will also admit that years ago (many years ago), when Bottega Veneta launched their first woven leather handbags—at that time a spectacular new breakthrough—I thought it was a passing trend and refused to get in. Sometimes it pays to wait a year to keep an eye on a trend before you commit, especially if you are considering a major purchase.

A person with a strong sense of self and of her own style is above trends.

Because trends are related directly to what's happening in the culture, you *do* feel left out if you're not into the trend and embarrassed if you are wearing it once it has become passé. However, these feelings are related to your age and confidence level. Teenagers have to look like their peer group; they are obsessed by it. The right outfit is crucial to them; being a trendsetter and style maker is a hot position to hold. As you get older, you care less about what's "in" or what everyone else is wearing. This is also related to confidence; as you age, you develop your own look and learn to move forward with it rather than look backward over your shoulder at the latest twist in a fashion cycle.

Picking Trends

Each of us can only pick the trends that we can adapt to our own lives; we will latch onto an item, a look, or a silhouette based on what looks and feels right for our personal style. Out of a shopping bag full of trends, ranging from pierced navels to cropped sweaters to jodhpurs and jeweled mules, maybe only jeweled mules will appeal to you or work with any aspect of your wardrobe. Picking the right trends for your lifestyle requires an editing process that hopefully will prevent you from becoming a fashion victim.

I have sort of a flamboyant personal style and like being a little ahead and a little over the top. I usually follow trends but also like to think that I can create my own. I have a signature accessory I depend on (series of bangle bracelets), so I'm usually looking at trends in terms of shape, color, or fun. Out of each season, I will possibly adapt only one or two new looks.

Yes, I bought that marabou-trimmed sweater because it's hot and it made me laugh and is meant to amuse others. But I also try to adapt trends to make them my own. I like to be inspired and to borrow from the fashion magazines, to test items for size and strength.

I recently saw a model in a French fashion magazine whose nails showed contrast tips and moons. I thought tips and moons were too much, but I liked part of the package, so I asked my manicurist to paint just moons. I had to show her how to do it, and the other manicurists gathered round to watch. Most chorused "ugly" while I beamed. (I guess moons aren't big in Korea.)

There's a subtle thrill of knowing you're on to something that will be on *every*one's lips—or hips—in a few months' time. It doesn't even have to be a major statement. Back to my manicure for a minute.

I read a *Women's Wear Daily* report from the couture collections in Paris. Both Dior and Givenchy have shown the same color nail varnish for fall. No one else has anything like this color, so

WWD calls it a trendlet; it's a wait and see. However, I see the picture and immediately bond with the color. It talks to me, and talks now—I don't want to wait for fall, I want it now. I go to my local drugstore, where I must sort through all the older bottles of polish to find what I am looking for. No current collection has anything like this—metallics and weird shades of blue, green, and yellow are being featured along with browns and aubergines—but way in the back, I find a single, dusty (honest) bottle of polish called Berry. It's as close as I can get without mixing my own, à la Hard Candy style. I buy the bottle, making a $4.69 investment. I am ambivalent, not jubilant.

While waiting to pay, I look at the bottle and have second thoughts about this color and almost leave it buried in the bubble gum at the front rack. What if someone sees me hiding it there? I pay.

"Gee, that's the ugliest polish I've ever seen," the saleswoman says to me as she rings up the purchase. That convinces me to press forward. If she hates it, it must be good.

I go home and do my nails. Bingo! The color is fabulous with my skin and feels better than good. I feel hot. I feel cutting edge. I feel like Superman with a manicure.

Even though no one else in America knows it, I know that this shade will be *the* in color for fall. I know this because when I tested it, it worked.

Trend Spin

Once a trend is in the air, it either takes hold or it doesn't. A trend that doesn't have legs will last only a season or a year and die—think of the pouf dress. RIP. It's quite possible that this cargo pants look will come and go, especially at the higher end. It's really a teen thing, no matter what Karl Lagerfeld says.

A trend with legs keeps on ticking and even reinvents itself into richer textures and better layers. Trends sometimes last longer than anyone (even in the trade) would have imagined. For example, the popularity of sheer and almost-transparent fabrics took root and grew in ways that astonished the trade. Eventually it will go the way of all trends, but it was a trend worth getting into early from a consumer point of view because those clothes could have been worn for more than three years and still looked very current.

Trends that don't work on real people don't make it.

I first caught onto this trend from reading *Women's Wear Daily* and decided to invest in a sheer slip dress under which I could layer another, less sheer slip. The few that I saw in stores cost several hundred dollars—more than I wanted to gamble. But at the end of the first season, when this look was just being carried by outré designers and the like, I found one of these dresses on the markdown rack at Filene's Basement. It had a hole in it; several buttons were off the back. It was pale pink, but it was filthy. It was marked down from $235 to $75.

I took this rag over to the Customer Service desk. I explained the weak points of the dress and said it simply wasn't worth $75. "How about $25?" the service rep asked me. Sold!

I teamed the dress with a man's gray pinstripe vest bought at Goodwill for $15—this covered the back where the hole was. I moved the existing matching buttons to the lower portion of the dress and filled in with spare buttons on the parts where the vest would cover the back. I wore pale pink tights, yellow socks cuffed with lace, and lavender suede slingback wedgies. I wore this outfit to several parties and even a job interview. I felt fabulous in it because I had taken a trend early on and twisted it, tweaked it, combined it with vintage, and made it mine.

Within the next year, when transparent was a serious trend with big legs, I found a tunic sweater to go with the dress and wore it that way. I had outgrown the look with the vest. The third year I found an underskirt and a linen jacket and wore that. A trend should evolve in your closet as it evolves in the stores and takes root stylistically.

I am still wearing this dress and adapting it, because sheer has stayed in fashion. I have also bought more transparent clothes and even now have bought fabric to make another.

There's usually a lag of six or seven months from when you spot a trend in a designer fashion show to when you will actually wear it.

The beauty of a solid trend is that it moves up a technological ladder and gets more sophisticated in subtle ways with each season. The sports look becomes the sports look in fastenings and closures in another season. Padded skirts become quilted jackets, which beget quilted handbags, an already old standby. What goes around comes around with just a little boost from the street and the catwalk.

Antitrend Traffic

When a trend threatens to overtake the country, or even a segment of it, there are many women who stand back and say, "Whoa. Wait a minute!" Even if they love the trend, they refuse to get on the bandwagon. Following trends—especially at a certain time in the trend's life—may give out the message that you are a follower without any mind or will of your own. That's why it's better on get on a trend early or to avoid trends totally.

Test Your Trend Affinity

How trendy do you need to be? Take this little quiz and test your flexibility.

1. My shopping style is (refer to page 9):
    A) Helter-Skelter
    B) Architectural or EuroSpender
    C) Conservative

2. My business is:

   A) fashion and the arts

   B) casual/wear anything

   C) extremely corporate

3. I get bored with what I look like:

   A) constantly

   B) every now and then

   C) every few years

4. My basic wardrobe colors are:

   A) this year, gray

   B) black

   C) neutrals

5. When I think about trying a new look, I am:

   A) excited

   B) wary

   C) frightened

6. My wardrobe is:

   A) a work of art

   B) somewhat flexible

   C) pretty much set

7. When I look at fashion magazines:

   A) I want everything

   B) I get a few ideas that are interesting

   C) I rarely read fashion magazines

8. When a trend suddenly appears everywhere:

   A) I've already been on it for at least a season

   B) I watch it to see if it will become something serious

   C) who cares—most trends are stupid

9. At the beginning of the major seasons, I go to my closet and:

   A) weed out the stuff that's "out"

   B) organize everything by color

   C) clean

10.   At the end of the season, I go to my closet and:
      A) put away items for my fashion collection
      B) make a pile of things to take to the consignment shop or to
         give away
      C) clean

To score yourself: If you have mostly A answers, you have a high need to move onto the next trend; if mostly B answers, you are aware of trends but take them in your stride and don't get overly excited; if mostly C answers, you have little interest in trends.

Do It Yourself

I use my own limited sewing and crafting skills in the smaller fashion and trend items, the things where a little do-it-yourself experimentation goes a long way. I want you to know that I have disasters all the time. I throw things away. I ruin things. I'm not Martha Stewart. But I am more than capable of sewing velvet ribbon to an inexpensive cardigan to create a homegrown version of those pricey Voyage tops that were the rage—and save $500 while I'm at it. I can make an A-line skirt or a headband, or change cheap buttons for vintage buttons to upgrade an otherwise inexpensive piece of junk.

Even if you have a failure in a do-it-yourself trend adaptation, this failure can teach you how intricate the process is—and how much the effect is worth to you at the retail level. The harder a trend is to copy at home, the more likely it will succeed in stores. People don't like to buy things they can do themselves; they don't want to feel ripped off or cheated into buying something that they could easily make if they had the time and supplies.

Those Voyage-like cardigans I was making? Would you believe I had to take the first one apart because I couldn't get the velvet ribbon to follow the curve of the neckline properly and still lie flat? Applying the trim was harder than it looked…as are most of the couture details that become trendy.

One of the easiest trends to adapt has been the vintage-lingerie look and the camisole rage. About five years ago I read that Stella McCartney (the daughter of Paul) was buying up vintage slips from the flea markets in London. McCartney had been to design school and was then working for a Savile Row tailor. By combining a man-tailored suit with a camisole created from these old slips she created a sexy new look that caught on immediately, earning her her own line before she moved on to replace Karl Lagerfeld as the designer for the Chloe line in Paris. Good goin', Stella! As soon as you visualize her concept, you know she's right on target.

The moral of the story is to look at what the creative types are doing and see if there's even a nugget of an idea in there that you can adapt yourself. Once Stella showed me the way, I didn't have to be a genius. I can go to the flea market, buy an old slip, cut it off, and wear it with a suit. I can even dye the slip as Stella does, though I stop short of beading, which she does, too, but then she's Stella and I'm not.

The basic idea of man-tailored clothing with softly feminine slips makes sense. That's why the trend caught on. Not all trends make sense, but you could see this one coming from four thousand miles away. Furthermore, it was a trend that had something for everyone—indeed, an entire industry sprang up at local crafts fairs of women who had rushed out and bought up old slips and cut them into camisoles.

Original Sin

Just don't carry the do-it-yourself theme too far. Or test your talents, learn them, and stick to the learned message. If you can't make the item as well as they make it in the store, don't go out in public with the homemade version.

Many years ago, back in the dark ages when I was first in the fashion business, Ralph Lauren began making women's wear and did a collection of skirts created from old American quilts. They were stunning but caused quite a stir with collectors who said it was a sin to cut up a quilt simply to make a garment from it.

Since I collect quilts, I had to give this argument a lot of thought. I finally decided that there was such a thing as the Rule of Original Sin. It is a sin to cut up and destroy a perfectly good anything: blanket, quilt, whatever. However, if the item is in such bad shape that it is beyond repair or beyond representing its own kind in its original form, then it's perfectly acceptable to "destroy" it and let it rise from the ashes like the phoenix as entirely new.

With this philosophy, I cut up a damaged quilt and made a dress and jacket that I have to this day—it's stunning and special. This adventure in trend following was 100 percent successful.

A lot of the time—on one of your shopping escapades in the attic, perhaps, or in a vintage boutique—you'll discover something that's interesting but not right. The style has indeed come back into vogue, but the example you own is not on target enough to make you feel triumphant. Once again you realize that, yes, everything does come back again, but it comes back in a somewhat different form.

At this point you must decide if you should "do something" to the item. You must decide if it's dead in the attic and useless or if it can pay you dividends if you update it and modify it to meet a current style or trend. This is tricky, because if you send it out to a pro it will cost money, may not be right when finished, and you will have thrown good money after bad when you could have bought something new that you loved.

If you take on the project yourself, you can botch it. Don't think that everything has worked out as well as my quilt project or my Voyage-inspired cardigans. I once had two magnificent Calvin Klein skirts—they sat in the closet for years because they were out of style. (Don't laugh, but they were dirndls!) They were made of gorgeous and expensive and very chic fabric. I got the brilliant idea that I should cut them off their waistbands and add them to a skirt yoke that would drop the length and change the style per the new requirements of fashion. Since they weren't doing anything positive for me in the closet, I figured "what the hell" and began to cut and sew.

Examine trends and then figure out how to copy them before investing in something expensive that could be a great do-it-yourself project.

I will not bore you with the specifics or the enormity of this disaster. I will tell you that twelve years later, I still get ill remembering how I butchered that magnificent yardage. This memory has kept me from making further mistakes in the do-it-yourself department and to reevaluate my definition of original sin.

My rule, growing out of that bad experience, has been to do

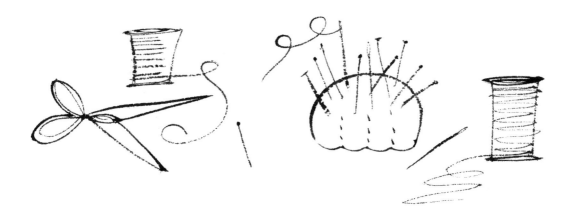

very little to anything I "buy" in my closet, even changing a hem length! This may sound incredibly conservative to you—and it is—but I learned the hard way that you can rarely alter one aspect of a garment without throwing all its proportions out of whack. Live with it as is, or leave it until it comes into its own again. Trendiness be damned!

chapter 9

Odds and Ends

Filling In Your Wardrobe

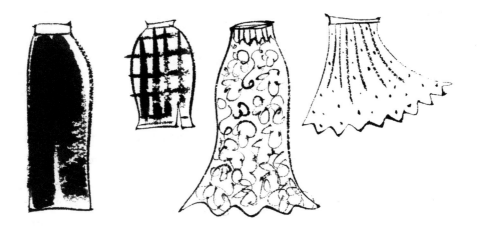

if what we wear is indeed the message we wish the world to receive, there's nothing to say we aren't allowed to change the message. You may want to change the message within a single day—we often do this when we take off our business clothes and slip into a pair of jeans ("Let me just slip into something a little more comfortable")—or you may want to gradually change the message as your personal tastes change. When you go out for the evening, you need to change the message; when you walk into a certain meeting—or even your high school reunion—you may want to modify your message.

It is often appropriate to rethink the signals we send: that's why we don't wear lace and sparkles to the office but adore to don them when the sun sets and a big date approaches. We go to a nightclub, to a wedding, on vacation, on a business trip, on a cruise (which has a very specific dress code and required dress for each night) and we need different types of clothes. In cases like this, the structure of the destination dictates that you change your message and prescribes how much latitude you have in making that change.

The point of dressing up or dressing for a special meeting or event is that you have permission to change the message you are sending through your clothes. With special occasion clothes, it's even more important than usual that you feel good about what you're wearing.

It's not unusual for a person to suddenly decide she's sick of what she looks like and to want to create a totally *new* image. In fact, we all probably like those makeover sections in magazines so much because we have within us the ability to shed a skin and grow a new one...figuratively speaking, of course. For someone with internal needs, I suggest going back to earlier chapters and using the magazine-clipping method to help hone a new Personal Style.

The Ages of Woman

Often changes in style are related to age and events. There's no question in my mind that age is a great liberator and gives you not only some freedom in what you wear but a lot of confidence to change your look and your statement to the public. I think it's a mistake to think there's such a thing as "looking your age."

Too old for a miniskirt? Tell that to Tina Turner!

Too old for body-conscious, curvy clothes? Tell that to Joan Collins!

Too old for long hair? Tell that to Gloria Steinem!

Adding on birthdays does not mean eliminating fun, fashion, or style from your wardrobe, nor does it mean eliminating styles you enjoy wearing. Adding the confidence and wisdom that comes with birthdays should help you extend and adapt your wardrobe. You may come to realize that being comfortable is more important than wearing stiletto heels. You may discover the joys of elastic waists and wrap skirts. You may reassess your dry-cleaning bill and decide that polyester blouses should replace silk in your closet. Some get the urge to pare down and simplify; others want to cut loose and amplify.

There are two forces that tell us to change our look—external (we're going out) and internal (we seek change from the inside out).

Never change a look or a wardrobe that works for you because you don't think it's age-appropriate.

I always thought that a woman became more and more sophisticated in her look as she aged. I expected to dress like my mother's friends did, since that is my basic frame of reference.

Instead, I've discovered that I feel so much more freedom at this stage in my life that I experiment with funky far more than I used to, that I have loosened up enormously and feel a freedom to express my personality and make an individual style statement that I could not make years ago when I needed the acceptance and support of the establishment more than I do today. As I head for a meeting tomorrow, I could wear a navy suit—but I think I'm going to wear a hot pink and coral silk print blouse and skirt ensemble that I bought at Anthropologie, a store that caters to teens and tweens.

We begin our professional wardrobe tentatively and conservatively; the directions we take after that depend on the roads taken and the whisper of the muses.

Age	Wardrobe Style
20–30	conservative; financially stretched
30–40	established; financially strong
40–50	peak confidence; financial peak
50–60	redefined; financially strong
60–70	refined and redefined physically and financially
70–100	comfort and style over price

Expansion on Sale

Once you have a strong wardrobe, the best way to expand it is to buy quality items on sale. Every now and then you need to evaluate a certain look and spring for it at full retail price, to enjoy it from the minute the season begins, but with careful planning and keen observation powers, you should rely on sales and off-price for most expansions.

The times that you should splurge for full retail are hopefully related to your personal organization, not disorganization (paying full price because you didn't get to planning ahead is bad business). But you have my permission to dive in when you are beginning your start-up wardrobe or when you are looking to make an important add-on, especially if the add-on has a touch of fashion to it. Because fashion is so perishable, you may as well pay a little more for it and enjoy it for a full run.

Things to buy at full price:

- chic shoes that are also *comfortable*
- a moderately priced jacket that doesn't look cheap and epitomizes a new trend (think fur trim)
- a black skirt of the moment

Never buy an item you don't need or don't love just because the price is right, especially if you intend to wear it for a special event.

Things to buy on sale:

- an extra blouse to go with your Gotcha Suit (see page 134), especially if it helps take the suit into evening wear
- a popular skirt silhouette that has already been successful for you in one color (buy other colors that coordinate and expand your existing core wardrobe)

Dress Up Through Accessories

There are plenty of books and guides that tell you to change your look with a scarf or a piece of jewelry. I love this idea but can't make it work for me. To me, accessories finish off and round out an outfit but do not serve to significantly make it into something

> *Accessories help to change the message; they alone can take you from day to night, from office to dinner.*

else. I don't tie up too much money in belts, bells, or whistles. But I always have on hand a few accessories that will take a basic and transform it from sporty to dressy. Indeed, that's why pearls were invented.

Adding on one hot accessory to an otherwise normal outfit can make it sing. When choosing accessories to expand your wardrobe, there are two ways to go:

1. cheap, trendy items that say "I'm hip"
2. expensive, quality items that are classics that say "I'm rich"

The rich look can actually pay for itself if you amortize a strong classic over a period of years; that's why the Hermès scarf is such a popular item. Some icon accessories worth saving up for that will pay you back over the years are:

- Chanel earrings—one pair gold tone; one pair pearl—approximately $150 per pair.
- Pair of designer faux gold-tone and diamond dress-up earrings or fake diamond studs of a reasonable size (not too big!)—expect to pay $150 for gold and diamond earrings.

- Shawl, chiffon stole, pashmina wrap, etc.
- High-quality fake pearl multistrand, about $200 to $250.
- Statement-of-style brooch, either an antique or vintage piece or something from a designer (sale) with colored stones, pearls, and diamonds, large enough to make an outfit go from plain to splendid.
- Fabulous evening bag, preferably not gold tone (see page 178) and hopefully bought on sale—designer is better, $100 to $200.

- Gold collar necklace in classic style, preferably real gold (18 karat, please), about $2,000. Lacking that kind of scratch, consider an excellent copy, $350 to $450. I'm not talking a chain or something flimsy, nor am I talking a copy of a designer style.

Travel

Travel is both a science and an art; looking right for every destination is usually a learned skill that takes a lot of thought and planning. A trip begins way before you leave for the airport. I begin to pack for any trip about a week before I leave, just to make sure I have all the pieces back from the cleaners, that everything fits into the type of suitcase I want to travel with, to decide if I've made the right choices. When I just throw and go, I invariably make mistakes.

Business Travel

Just about everyone has some business travel these days. Frequently, younger people break into a field by taking on jobs that require a tremendous amount of travel. Road warriors all develop their own style and tricks that work for them. Here are a few of mine:

1. Base the entire travel wardrobe on one color group that is keyed to shoes, just like your regular wardrobe. Note: black is the easiest but not the only choice. The shoes are chosen very specifically for the demands of the trip—if I'm driving a lot and going on short sales calls, I can wear a shoe with a heel, whereas if I have to walk all day, heels are out of the question. There should be two pairs of shoes in the same color but of different heel heights coordinated to your color group.

2. Pare down the items packed so that they can mix and match to expand, but never cut it too finely. A three-piece suit (jacket,

skirt, trousers) should be the mainstay of a travel wardrobe, but don't limit yourself to just these three pieces.

3. Always pack one emergency extra outfit. (You just never know what can happen.) If you are checking your luggage but have a tight connection, carry this outfit on the plane with you so that if your luggage doesn't make it, you still have a backup plan. Make sure there's an extra pair of panty hose included.

4. Always pack one dress-up dinner dress (preferably black) that can cover any dinner or cocktail invitation that comes at the last minute. Make sure you have the whole outfit—hose and shoes, earrings.

5. Make a checklist of your appointments and who you will see, decide how many times you can wear the same clothes (providing there are no spills or stains). The idea that you must wear a different outfit every day is outdated.

6. Consider fabric content when you pack. Are clothes more likely to wrinkle? Are they washable? If washable, will they dry overnight? Cottons usually do not dry overnight, whereas synthetic fibers do. Consider investing in a knit suit because knits travel so well. Learn a little about the types of knits; one with a "twist" in the fiber, such as a tricot, can be worn in just about any season. Beware, however, of knit silk and silk jerseys, which snag and will not hold up to the stress of travel.

7. Always travel with a small iron. Not all hotels have them in the room; it may slow you down to have to call housekeeping and then wait.

8. Always pack an umbrella, no matter what the weather; always pack a bathing suit, no matter what the weather. Always pack a pair of socks.

9. Do not travel with serious jewelry. Limit accessories because your time will be limited and you will not want to fool with bangles, beads, or scarf tricks. One pair of pearl and one pair of gold-tone earrings should do the trick; pearls are always good.

10. Dress for success on travel days. Airlines are more likely to upgrade you if you are professionally dressed. Besides, you never know who you'll meet. A trousers suit is comfortable and chic and appropriate for just about any trip. While looking nice is important, never travel in your best business clothes unless you must go directly into a meeting or public appearance. The stress of travel is hell on your clothes; fragile fabrics may not be up to it. Consider buying a suit that is your "travel suit"—mine is a polyester blend. I bought it at Loehmann's: it's a copy of a designer look that cost $225; it looks great and holds up well no matter what I do to it.

Leisure Travel

The rules of putting together a leisure travel wardrobe are obviously different and are related to the destination. I find that no matter how much research I do with guidebooks, magazine clippings, and the Internet, I still often misinterpret the "look" at that destination and go too casual. If I've learned anything for a well-rounded leisure travel wardrobe, it's to trade up my look and find some happy medium between casual and chic.

If the weather is going to be hot, I pack big baggy skirts or dresses but I *never* (no, never) wear shorts and T-shirts or the kind of clothes that I might wear while cleaning my attic. Even on vacation, there are ways to dress up and dress down at the same time and be a better version of you than if you completely let go.

For people who often visit the same destination on vacation, or destinations with a similar climate, it sometimes pays to invest in a wardrobe that is appropriate for that destination. The colors, the fabrics, the styles may be totally different in your vacation paradise—you could look like a fool in your own version of casual when there is a prescribed style of dress for that location. I spend a lot of time in the summer in the Mediterranean, which has a different kind of weather and a different style of dressing than in the New England village where I live the rest of the year. Over the years I have built a destination-specific wardrobe that stays in its own plastic bag in my attic until it's time to travel.

While the clothes are separated from my regular wardrobe, the shoes and accessories are not. I therefore leave a computer printout in the garment bag with the lists of shoes, bags, and accessories that mix and match with this wardrobe.

In Chapter 1 we discussed peer pressure and the need to tell the world that you are OK. The world you are addressing often changes when you travel, especially if you are on vacation. We've all been to places where the tourists stick out like a sore thumb or seen movies that visually poke fun at Americans abroad by depicting them as poorly dressed (no white socks with your sandals, please). Dressing as appropriate to local style will improve your comfort level. Yes, costume and wardrobe begin to merge here, but it won't be the first time.

If your travels take you on a cruise, you will find a new twist to the rules of building a travel wardrobe because most cruise ships—especially the large ones—have a dress code for each evening. Two or three nights at sea will be formal...then there are several terms that are very confusing because the definitions provided by the ships don't jibe with the words. For example, "informal" usually is very dressy—clothes appropriate for a country club.

Some people like to go on cruises because they have the chance to wear clothes they rarely get to wear. I always have a good chuckle looking over the crowd on formal night to see how many obvious mother-of-the-bride dresses have been trotted out for one more wearing. Some people fret over the clothes required for the cruise; others have as much fun shopping for clothes for the cruise as they will have on the cruise itself.

Calling Coco Chanel

When I started to travel a lot for business and needed to look authoritative at airline and hotel check-in desks, I invested in a real pair of gold-tone Chanel earrings with the double-C Chanel logo on them. Do not consider buying fakes; they reflect badly on you! While a pair of Chanel earrings costs about $150, they are an excellent investment in your future, as they tell the world that you have arrived.

It does not pay to invest in a cruise wardrobe on your first cruise. See how you like the lifestyle first; then, if you will take more cruises, keep an eye out for the items you will need to balance your cruise wardrobe. If you enjoy cruising on a regular basis, you know there will be a certain number of formal nights in your year, and you can watch for good bargains throughout the year.

Special Occasion Clothes

Over the years we develop a collection of party dresses, Little Black Dresses, and maybe even "formals" or ball gowns, depending on lifestyle and need. I happen to believe that every young woman's prom dress should be a Little Black Dress so that she'll have it for college years and her start-up wardrobe, but most young women prefer to have trendy statements for their first dress-up dates and then invest in a proper Little Black Dress when they begin to build a proper wardrobe.

Because special occasion clothes are not worn often, some people prefer to buy inexpensive outfits. While this works for teenagers and young women, by the time you are in the workforce, it's time to rethink your wardrobe and your dress-up look.

Most women should be able to take advantage of sales and markdowns to buy their special events outfits. Don't wait for the invitation to arrive in the mail—by then, the pressure is on. Buy your first Little Black Dress as strategically as possible; one dress-up outfit that is not black should also hang in your closet, ready at a moment's notice.

When shopping for dress-up clothes, remember these facts:

1. The biggest problem with dress-up clothes is length, since various hem lengths come into style. As you grow your dress-up wardrobe, you should be mindful of skirt lengths and add in one trousers suit or at least a pair of tuxedo pants or dressy silk or satin pants that can be dressed up or down. In fact, dress-up separates are worth considering, so that a camisole can dress up a business suit; a blazer or dinner jacket with metallic threads or pearl buttons can be added to existing pieces, or the tuxedo trousers can be matched with your crew neck black sweater and a shawl for a classic look.

2. Choose classic styles appropriate for many wearings, hopefully over years. Think chic, yet don't buy anything that shouts "look at me," because once everyone has looked, everyone will remember what you wore and you will not want to wear it too often. Almost invisible is the real chic.

3. Don't pick clothes that are too sexy or explicit. The most sexy clothes cover the body anyway. While you will want the clothes to be soft and feminine, you do not want them to announce every nuance that lies beneath the dress. It's bad manners and bad style.

4. Consider what's called a "dinner suit"—it's not flashy but is very practical, and a wise choice can last a decade, or longer. A dinner suit has three pieces and is dressier than a day suit, with maybe pearl or jewel buttons or trims, but it isn't too dressy and therefore is appropriate for everything from dinner to cocktails to black tie.

5. Include a "wrap" in the ensemble investment; I hate a glam look teamed with a raincoat. Invest in a shawl, evening jacket, or appropriate cover-up for nights out. Likewise, you will need the right shoes and handbag.

Evening clothes last longer when they are of classic styles and simple lines. To avoid mistakes, consider this list of "don'ts":

1. Don't buy beaded ensembles while building a wardrobe—more things can go wrong with beads than right. If the beading isn't of good quality, it can cheapen your wardrobe; the beads can also fall off or leave "holes" in the garment. Beaded outfits are difficult—and expensive—to clean. If you want beads, try to keep it simple.

2. Don't team a quality garment with cheap-looking shoes and evening bag. When bought carefully evening shoes (and bag) need not be expensive, but they should look good and keep the style on par.

Make investments in quality that lasts—again, choose style, not fashion—and pick clothes that will last many, many years so they can pay you back. A well-chosen Little Black Dress should last ten to twenty years.

3. Don't put a lot of money into seasonal fabrications, unless you continually wear dress-up clothes during the same season.
4. Don't buy something because it's handy, well priced, or practical—if you don't love it, you will never feel glamorous in it, and the whole point of getting dressed up is to step outside your everyday life and into another world, if only for a few hours.
5. Don't wear the bridesmaid dress that you are trying to amortize.

Unexpected Places to Find Dress-up Accessories

- your boyfriend's or husband's closet (adjustable tux tie)
- grocery store (lunch box as evening bag)
- hardware store (tackle box or fishing basket as evening bag)
- home furnishings discount store (lap blanket or chenille throw as shawl)
- craft store or silk flower supply warehouse (netting, ribbon, silk flowers, glitter)

Weddings

Until the day she died, my mother never forgave her mother-in-law for one sin. You see, Grandma Jessie wore a white suit to my parents' wedding. Tradition has it that only the bride wears white. I mention this because last night I went to a wedding. The bride happened to have planned a white-on-white wedding, so her attendants were wearing white, as were all the parents. But I was shocked when I counted five other guests who were wearing white. Hey guys, get a life! No one wears white but the bride and whomever she tells to wear white. End of story.

Other than that, there are no hard-and-fast rules, although what you wear to a wedding (when you are not the bride) is dependent on the time of day, the dress code requested by the bride, and the customs in that community.

Go to a wedding in England or Australia and you really need a terrific hat (rent the video-cassette of *Four Weddings and a Funeral* for a fashion lesson on the look). Few women in American wear hats anymore, even to weddings, but if you love the look, a wedding is the one place you can get away with it and not look or feel like an idiot.

When possible, get the local rules of dress from people who live in the area and gather information from more than one source.

Just as you may not wear white, you should not pick any clothing that has a "look at me" subtext to it. All eyes are to be on the bride; it's her day. Whether you're attending the wedding so you can be the next bride or not, anything that attracts too much attention to you is the wrong choice.

Should you fall into the time of your life when you are attending a lot of weddings, it may be worthwhile to invest in an outfit to wear or to work into your wardrobe budget the kinds of clothes that are appropriate to wear to day weddings that can also be woven into your business wardrobe. Evening weddings should be addressed with your dress-up wardrobe.

It is perfectly acceptable to wear black to an evening wedding. Dressy trousers suits are also acceptable.

Funerals

It's not considered polite to think about death or to plan for funerals, yet they are a part of the life cycle. Being prepared to go to a funeral at a moment's notice is part of having a smart wardrobe. For the most part, a dark-colored suit is appropriate—it need not be black. A simple silk dress is also OK. More and more people wear trousers to both weddings and funerals. In fact, many of the rules for weddings also apply to funerals.

The choice of a hat at a funeral usually has to do with religious rituals, not style statements—you often must have your head covered so that a hat, a mantilla, or a scarf needs to be available to you.

Funeral gear to always have hanging in the closet:

- simple dark suit
- simple dark dress for hot weather
- dark shoes and stockings to match
- black or navy hat or mantilla

Big Dates

Whether it's the prom, your high school reunion, or simply dinner with your honey, you will enjoy it more if you give your wardrobe some special attention. The secret to feeling good about yourself for a special event is to give yourself enough time to prepare. Preparation should begin way before the date, and I don't mean allowing yourself an hour for a bath and makeup, I mean making a ritual out of choosing the garments, the accessories, the makeup, and the coiffure, then giving yourself enough time in your schedule to get dressed and dolled up at a leisurely pace.

For a special event, time to prepare is as important an element as the dress, the shoes, and the hairdo.

Even if you are having a fit of second doubts about what you have chosen, understand that what you are wearing isn't that important—it's how you feel. Since it's too late now to change the choice, making yourself crazy can only damage your mental health and ruin the evening. Give yourself a talking-to, readjust your attitude, stand up straight, breathe deeply, and go out there and smile. Good posture and a big smile are the most important accessories you can ever take to a special event. And they are both free.

When the event is over, you'll discover that what you wore didn't really matter. You could have gone in a five-year-old black dress and it wouldn't have mattered much. What did matter was your smile, your confidence, and your attitude. Use clothes and accessories to help you fine-tune these, but use yourself to put your best foot forward. Cinderella will have nothing over you.

Item/qty		Times Worn		
		per week	per month	per year